New Techniques for
5 STRING BANJO

Volume 2 - Beyond Beginner
Journeyman/Journeywoman

JEFF BELDING

Editing by: Ronny Schiff

Formatting by: Edwina Belding

Cover Design by: www.fiverr.com/josepepitojr

ISBN 978-0-578-77107-6

More information about the audio access that accompanies this book
is available at www.jeffbelding.com

Dedication

This book is dedicated to Roger Sprung and Bill Keith,
two banjo teachers who inspired me to pursue this instrument to its fullest.

One of the many Roger Sprung albums in
my collection.

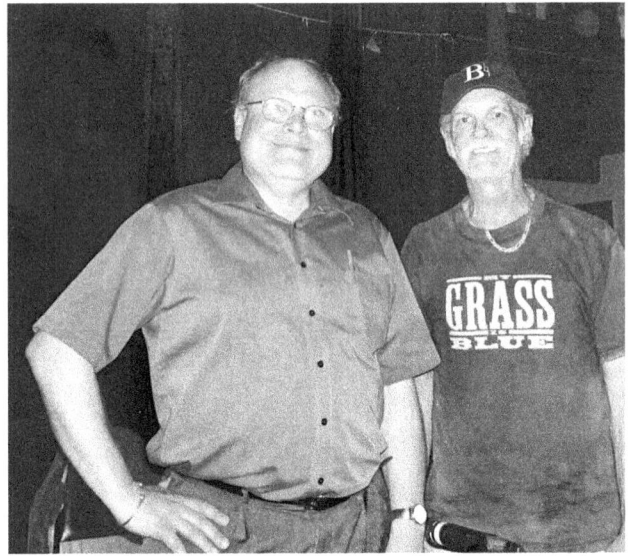

With Bill Keith at the Colony in
Woodstock, NY 2006

Also dedicated to the family I grew up with and lost —
and to the family I have now, to assure me I will never be alone.

Acknowledgment

To my wife, Edwina for all her hard work to make my dream of becoming an author a reality!

Table of Contents

Introduction

In early March 2019, a package arrived at our little "flat" in Phoenix. It contained some copies of my (then) new book, *New Techniques For 5 String Banjo, Volume 1, Beginner.*

The die was cast. I was sitting on a pile of copies of my first book, wondering…"Okay, this is all well and good, and I'm proud of my accomplishment, but, *Now What!*" So on that very same day, I set right to work on *New Techniques For 5 String Banjo, Volume Two…better late than never!*

My biggest fans back in my home state of New York were already asking, "So, when is Volume Two coming out?" The best answer I could give any of these folks was, "Sometime in 2020." You see by now, they had been taught by me, *all* the things that were in the first book. They were already hungry for more!

I had a feeling that the answer I gave them was rather disappointing, but I "was where I was" in this long term project. All I could do was to pound this thing out as quickly as I could, while still adhering to the following principles of my teaching philosophy:

- There is *no such thing* as being *too* careful about explaining musical concepts. In the countless times I spent in front of a banjo class, I could *always* tell by the faces in the crowd, that what I just said flew right past them, and they needed more explanation! That is why in these pages that follow, you may read something and think, "Hey! He already mentioned that in the last chapter!" To me, important musical concepts bear repeating again and yet *again!*

- Play accompaniment for your students *often*. Since I began this journey back in the late '70's, this has *always* been one of the cornerstones of my teaching philosophy. This second book includes *vast* amounts of accompaniment in the audio companion. If I can't be in the room with you physically you have my "digital presence" playing those back-up chords to help you with your musical presentations.

- Be encouraging to the *extreme!* If there is any *one* thing that I like to point out about teaching a musical instrument, it would be to leave *no stone unturned* when it comes to keeping students engaged! All too often, students get discouraged, saying something like, "I just don't know if I have the talent for this. I may never be able to pull this 'music-making' thing off!" At this point you might ask, "How can an instruction book be encouraging to folks with these kinds of concerns?" For one thing, this book puts every tune it presents under an "electron microscope." From a simple melody to a challenging variation, there is a *careful process* to get you from the bottom rung of the ladder, up to the top. Granted, that final variation may take awhile to fully absorb. That's okay! Move on to the easy version of the *next* tune and live to play that extra-challenging piece another day.

The free audio companion is also a way that this book can give encouragement to the student. I personally prefer audio to video so that you can look at the book and the neck of the banjo without distraction. That is the power that these many hours of audio recordings provide for you! If you're looking for encouragement, believe *me*, you will find it there!

Upon completing this project, I've done my best to adhere to these beliefs. Plus, a Glossary is included for terms with which you may not be familiar. *New Techniques For 5 String Banjo, Volume 2, Beyond Beginner* may be challenging in places, but I believe you will find that it strikes a balance between "serious music talk" and just plain "Good Pickin' *Fun!*"

Other Books by Jeff Belding
available at _amazon.com_

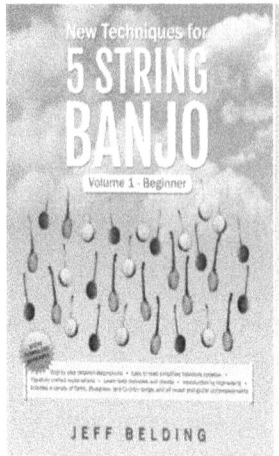

New Techniques for 5 String Banjo
Volume 1 Beginner

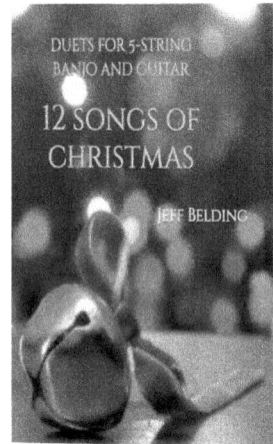

12 Songs of Christmas—Duets for
5 String Banjo and Guitar

If you purchased any of my books through Amazon I'd appreciate it if you would post a helpful, relevant review on Amazon based on your honest opinion and experience.

Thanks for your purchase!

You can contact me at jeff.belding@yahoo.com with comments and questions.

The audio "companion" for this book can be accessed through my website www.jeffbelding.com or directly on YouTube at the
New Techniques for 5 String Banjo channel.

CHAPTER 1

SOME REVIEW OF VOLUME 1 CONCEPTS

How to Read Jeff's Version of Banjo Tablature (For more, see Volume 1, pages 10—15)

- Tab Staff: Top line, D or 1st string, followed by B or 2nd, G or 3rd, D or 4th, and High G or 5th, bottom line.

- Measures: Most banjo tablature is broken down into *measures* of eight beats or the equivalent (each beat is an eighth note or an eighth note "pause").

- Frets: Each note in a measure is marked with a number (*zero* for an open string) to show which fret to play on a particular beat (Volume 1, page 11).

- Strings: On whatever line on the Tab staff a fret number appears, it tells you which string to pick while holding down that fret on *that* particular string.

- x: An "x" on the center line of the Tab staff denotes a pause of one eighth note beat in length.

- R: An "R" denotes a *longer* pause worth two eighth notes in length (R = xx).

- Eighth notes: Appear as numbers on the Tab staff "one after the other" with no spaces or pauses in-between.

- Quarter notes: Appear as a number on the Tab staff followed by an "x."

- Half notes: Appear as a number on the Tab staff followed by an "x" and an "R."

- Pinch: Two or more notes picked simultaneously.

Picking and Fretting Hand Markings

The Picking Hand

- Thumb: "TH"—Picks 3rd, 4th, or 5th strings.

- Index: "I"—Picks only 2nd string (until further notice...).

- Middle: "M"—Picks only the 1st string (until further notice...).

- Index finger picking exception: Index finger picks 3rd (and sometimes 4th) string when preceded by a thumb-picked eighth note on the 5th string.

- Picking hand markings (TH, I, and M) appear below the Tab staff. For the most part, it is assumed that the standard "Picking Hand Rules" apply. Picking hand markings occur when more unusual picking patterns are called for. Therefore, not every note has a picking hand marking.

The Fretting Hand

- Index: "ind"—Frets the first fret on *any* string.

- Middle: "mid"—Frets the second fret on *any* string.

- Ring: "ring"—Frets the third fret on *any* string.

- Pinky: "pink"—Frets the fourth or fifth fret on *any* string.

These markings (ind, mid, ring and pink) appear *above* the Tab staff, especially if unusual fretting hand situations take place. Any frets beyond the fifth fret are marked with a suggested fretting hand fingering.

For more in-depth review, see Volume 1, pages 16–20.

Review of All Chords Used in Volume 1 For more on interpreting chord diagrams see Volume 1, page 24. For useful chord review, try the following pages from Volume 1: Pages 25, 26 and 27; Page 34, Letter D; Page 37; Page 40; Page 53; Page 65, last 4 measures; Pages 75-76.

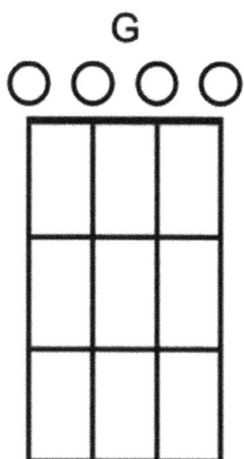

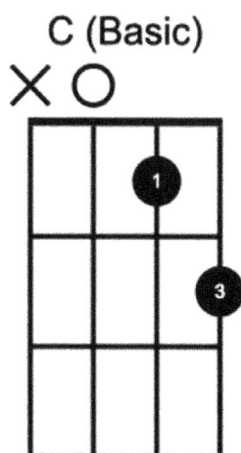

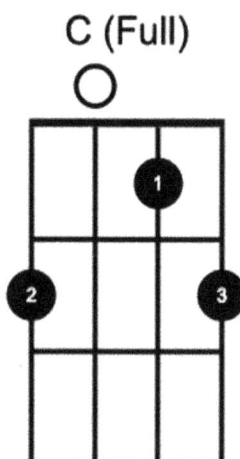

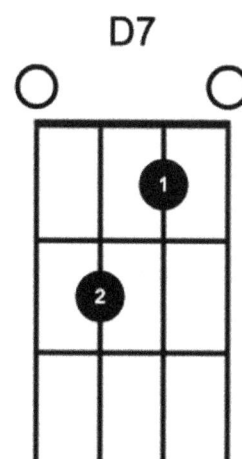

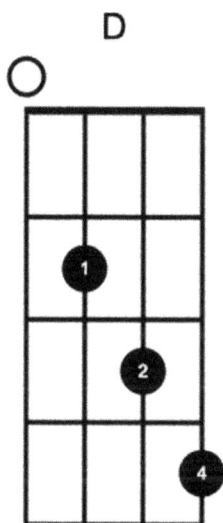

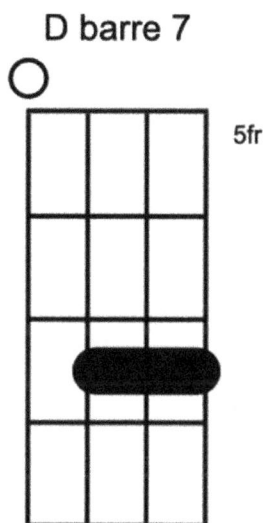

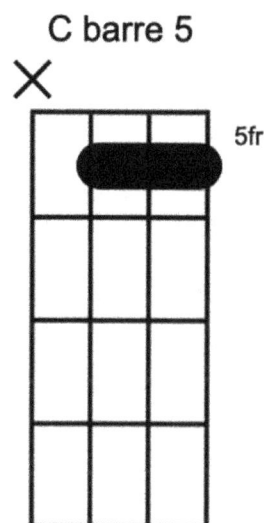

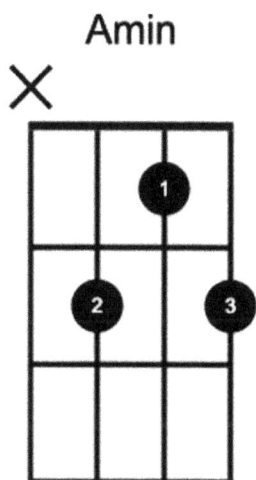

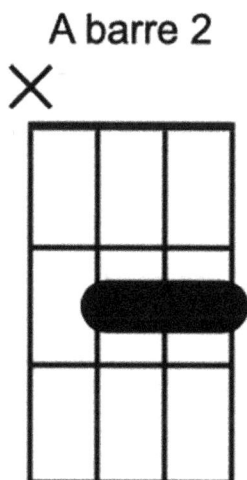

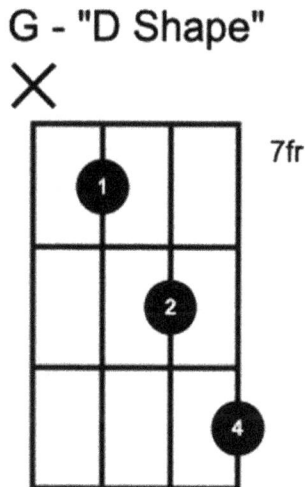

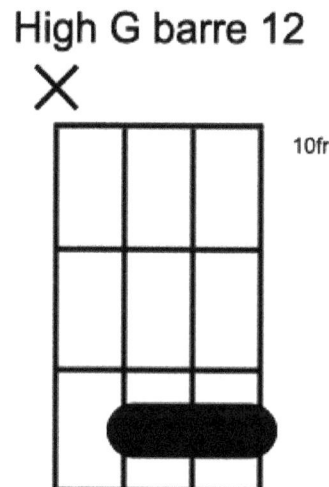

G

C (Basic)

C (Full)

D7

D

D barre 7
5fr

C barre 5
5fr

Amin

A barre 2

G - "D Shape"
7fr

High G barre 12
10fr

Review of Non-Picking Maneuvers

1) Hammer-ons   2) Pull-offs   3) Slides   4) Combinations

Suggestion: Review Volume 1, Pages 41 and 42.

16th Notes:

Two 16th notes fit in the space of one eighth note. Any two 16th notes almost always come in the form of a non-picking maneuver.

Marking for Two 16th Notes $\left(\wedge \right)$

1) Slide   2) Hammer   3) Hammer/Pull   4) Hammer

For more 16th note review, see Volume 1, Page 48 and Page 69, measures 29–44.

Three Widely-Used Time Signatures

- 4/4 ("Four-Quarter")—Four quarter notes or eight eighth notes per measure or the equivalent.

- 3/8 ("Three-Eighth")—Three eighth notes per measure or the equivalent. Often used in Irish jigs.

- 3/4 ("Three-Quarter")—Three quarter notes or six eighth notes per measure, or the equivalent.

- Also known as "Waltz Time."

Time signatures appear in regular music notation at the beginning of the top line of a piece of music. They don't show up on a Tab staff, so if it is in 3/8 or 3/4 time, you will be alerted in the text before a piece.

If there is no mention of a time signature of a tune, then you should *assume* it is in 4/4 time.

For more on time signatures, see Volume 1, pages: 38 (text at top); 51 (first paragraph); 52 (text at bottom).

Repeats and Jumps

1) Repeats:

Repeat to very beginning

Repeat section within the dots

Repeat previous measure

2) Skips & Jumps:

Second time: Skip 1 and go directly to 2.

First and Second Endings

1.   **2.**

First time: play to here and repeat

Banjo Rolls

A banjo roll is a repeating picking hand pattern that occurs on four or more separate strings. They can appear several *different* times within a tune and, can even occur four or more times in a *row* within a tune.

Two of these banjo rolls were given names in Volume 1:
- The Basic Scruggs Roll (Volume 1, page 25): This is a four beat repeating pattern.
- The Forward/Backward Roll (Volume 1, page 26): This is an eight beat repeating pattern.

Holding down various chords while playing a banjo roll is one of the primary characteristic sounds of a 5 string banjo. These characteristic sounds are called "arpeggios."

Here are 77 different banjo rolls taken from Volume 1 in the order in which they appeared. They are presented here as exercises on open strings, but try the patterns while holding down some of your basic chords as well.

- Notice that four-string banjo rolls repeat themselves *twice* in a measure.

- Also notice that some banjo rolls include pauses.

- Standard picking hand rules apply (see Chapter 1, page 8).

77 Banjo Rolls (From Volume 1)

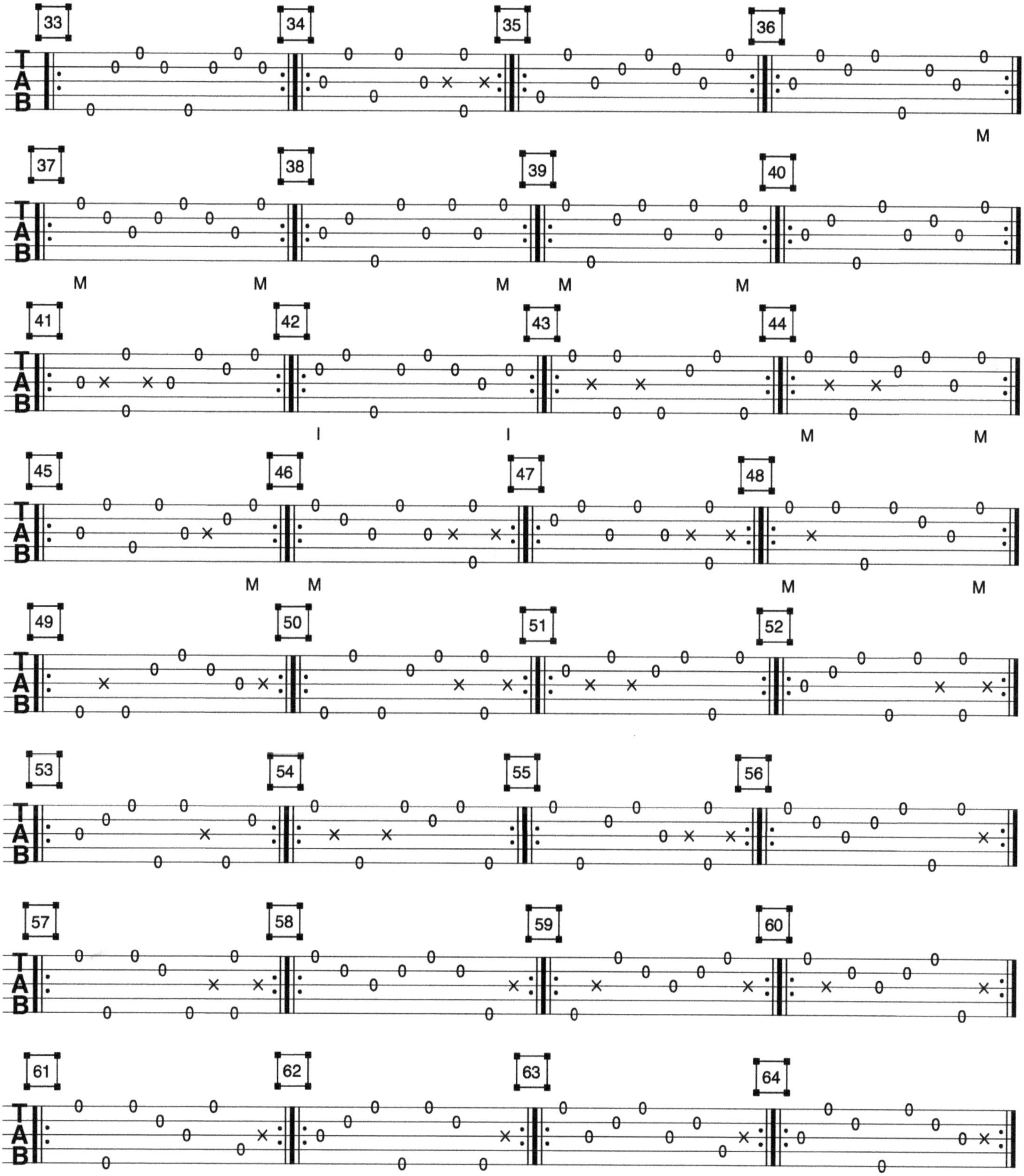
33 34 35 36
37 38 39 40
41 42 43 44
45 46 47 48
49 50 51 52
53 54 55 56
57 58 59 60
61 62 63 64

(Continues)

3/4 Time Banjo Roll from "Home on the Range" (Volume 1, Page 52, measure 31)

Review of Endings ("Tags") from Volume 1

These are endings for tunes in the key of G somewhat in the order of difficulty.

1) Basic "Shave and a Haircut"

2) Same fill as #1 with added "pinches"

Double Endings (4 measures each):

3) Used for "Oh! Susanna" and other tunes in the key of G.

4) Used for "Red River Valley," "Blue Ridge Cabin Home" and similar songs.

For the sake of variety, here's two more:

5)

6)

CHAPTER 2

THREE EASY BANJO INSTRUMENTALS TO "GET YOU GOING"

Here are three tunes of mine that are simple and straight forward in their rhythm and fingering. You will find examples of half, quarter, eighth and sixteenth notes, and some good review of basic chords and barres. If they're too easy, then try them once each and move on. It's a good way to "dust off" your banjo, if you've been away from it for awhile.

You could also use these tunes as part of your daily warm up. You should always start your practice sessions with something simple to "get you in the groove." Reading through these pieces can give you some heads-up on how my notation works, as well as getting your picking and fretting hands coordinated.

Enjoy!

Full color stickers of this dude for your banjo case are available for sale.
For more info visit jeffbelding.com

1) Nuts and Bolts

Standard picking hand rules apply: See Chapter 1, Page 8

By Jeff Belding

2) This Here Banjer

By Jeff Belding

3) An Evening With The Ziffels

By Jeff Belding

(*Implied - Banjo doesn't hold
C chord, but accompanist plays C.)

CHAPTER 3

"CRIPPLE CREEK" AND THE CAPO

If you have been through all of Volume 1 of this series, you may have noticed that the subject of the capo was not presented. It just didn't seem like the appropriate time to delve into this added layer of knowledge. There's plenty of repertoire to take in, without the extra dimension of involving the use of a capo.

What is a Capo?

The definition of a capo is:

(*noun*) A clamp fastened across all the strings of a fretted musical instrument to raise their tuning by a chosen amount.

That *chosen amount* of pitch raising, depends on *which* fret the capo gets clamped.

Purchasing Recommendations

Capos come in all kinds of versions and brands. They range in price from $5.00 to $75.00 or more! Make sure that you ask specifically for a *banjo* capo. $25.00 or less should set you up with a decent one. The Shubb brand capo is well built and reasonably priced to boot.

A Transitional Tune To Take You into the World of the Capo — "Cripple Creek"

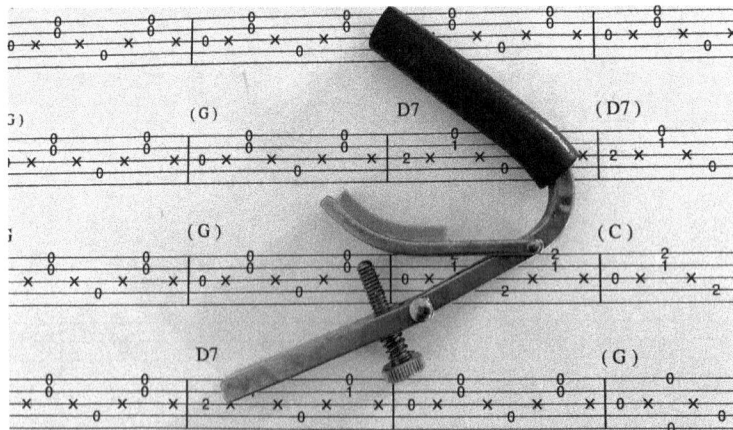

The Shubb capo

If you are playing "Cripple Creek" in a duet with a guitar, or in a group *without* a mandolin or fiddle, you can play it "as-is" in the key of G, *no* capo involved.

However, mandolin and fiddle players *always* play "Cripple Creek" (among dozens of other tunes) in the key of A. You may ask, "What do you mean by the key of G or the key of A?"

G — In Bluegrass, It's the "People's Key"

Start with the common key of G. Ninety percent of the time, the 5 string bluegrass banjo is tuned to G tuning as an all-open-string G chord. This is why so many songs and instrumentals played on the banjo are in the key of G.

The *chord* of G is "right in front of you." There is no effort needed to play a G chord. It is also worth noting that the open G chord contains half of the G major scale, once again with no effort needed or any need to involve your fretting hand. Then, by adding four fretted notes here and there, you have an *entire* G scale — more on this in the next chapter.

From playing the accompaniment for "Cripple Creek" (Volume 1, page 72), you should now be aware that the tune makes use of the three *primary chords* in the key of G. These three primary chords are: G, C, and D7.

Getting From G to A

The key of A is an acceptable "cheater's key" on your banjo, but how do you get there and what does this mean? If you remember "Home on the Range" from Volume 1, you learned an A barre chord for the accompaniment of *that* song (Volume 1, page 53). The A chord is a barre across the second fret.

Replacing the "human-finger barre" with a capo, second fret, you have created an "automatic" A chord.

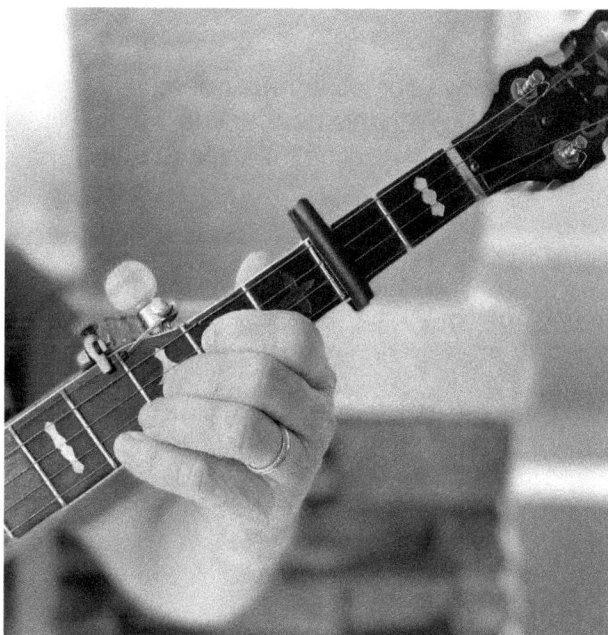

Capo 2nd Fret Front View

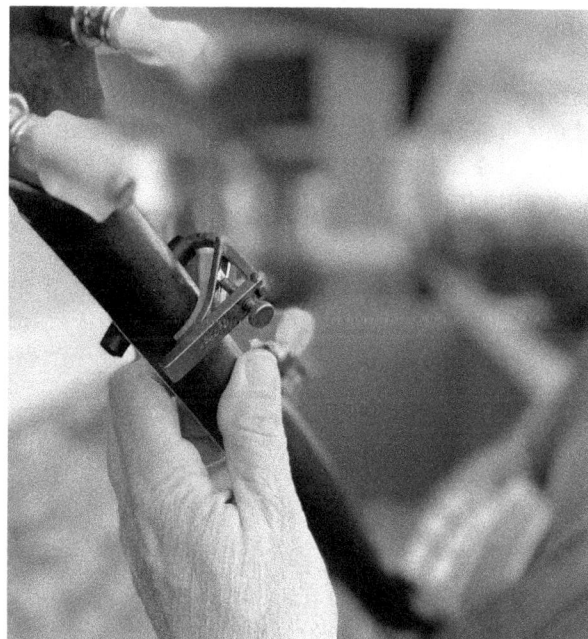

Capo 2nd Fret Rear view

You now have *transposed* your banjo's tuning from "G" to "A." The capo at second fret is how you "get there" but what is meant by calling this capoed key of A the "cheater's key?" It is because *every* string pattern, as well as the order of open strings versus fretted notes, and *every* chord position will look *identical* to the "Cripple Creek" that you played *without* the use of your capo.

You Are Not Done Yet!

The next step in this capo process, is to raise the short, fifth string G up (higher in pitch) to an A. This can be accomplished in three possible ways:

1) Tune the fifth string peg tighter until you arrive at A. Most fifth strings can handle this much tension, but there is no guarantee that it *won't* break on you. Certainly the fifth string can't be raised any *higher* than A, or that fifth string will surely be annihilated!

A Slight Music Theory Tangent

At this point you may be asking,"Why did you pick A, as the note for the fifth string?" I can explain it best in the following way:

As the high G or fifth string was to the open G chord, then high A is to the second fret, capoed (and now *open*) A chord. This way, the capo at second fret and the raised fifth string (to A) are now proportionally the *same* as when all the strings were *open* with no capo.

Two More Ways

2) Another way to achieve getting the fifth string up to high A, is to install a "railroad spike" at the seventh fret of the fifth string. The railroad spike is a little "hook" for the fifth string to be placed under, which raises the pitch of the fifth string to A, without the added strain of tuning the peg higher. Just a warning—unless you are very knowledgable about banjo neck anatomy, this is definitely a job for your music store repair technician.

3) You can also have a fifth string sliding capo installed on your banjo by your local "repair person." I use the Shubb fifth string capo, and have been very satisfied with it. With this device, you can capo the fifth string *anywhere* from the sixth to twelfth fret! For the key of A, slide the capo to the seventh fret and clamp it down.

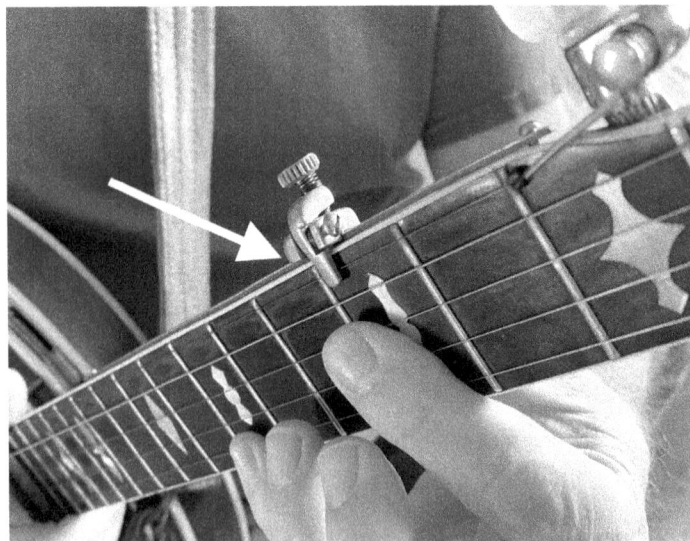

5th String Capo Clamped at 7th Fret

Another warning: The fifth string capo *does* add some width to the neck that you might find uncomfortable. It is probably a good idea to play a banjo with a fifth string capo to see how it feels before installing one on your *own* banjo. It's quite a "commitment" to have this device installed; so be forewarned!

Getting Close, But First, Another Music Theory Tangent *Is* Necessary

Okay, you have your capo on the second fret and your fifth string has been raised up to high A. All set for the key of A, right? NOPE! Make sure you check your tuning *again.* If you put on the capo without checking tuning, the banjo will sound kinda…horrible! Something to look out for when checking your tuning though…your tuner will show you a new and different series of notes than it did on the open strings. The read-out from the fifth string through the first is as follows:

A - E - A - C# (sharp) - E

If you stop and think about it, those new notes on your tuner's read-out, are alphabetically one letter further along than the notes *without* the capo. The capo at the second fret moves each original open string note one *whole step higher* as follows:

G (or 5th) becomes A (you might think H, but there is no musical note for H, and so H is *replaced* by A)
D (or 4th) becomes E
G (or 3rd) becomes A
B (or 2nd) becomes C#—more on *why* C is sharp (#) in the future
D (or 1st) becomes E

You Have Arrived!

So now that you have tuned up with your capo, you are ready to play "Cripple Creek" in A. Your *main* capo is the new "top of the neck," and your 5th string capo has been tuned up to A (see photo below). Other than knowing that, there is *nothing* else that you need to change.

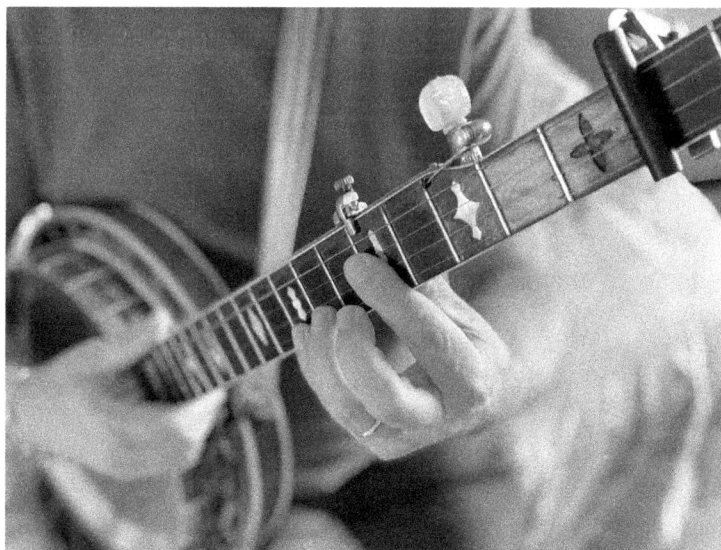

Both Capos Combined

All of the patterns, fretted notes, and chords will look *exactly the same.* You are just playing "Cripple Creek" *higher in pitch* as well as in the key of A. You might be a little thrown off because some of your fretboard dots and markers will be in different places, but you can adapt.

Back towards the beginning of this chapter, it was mentioned that the key of A is the "cheater's key" for banjo pickers. The reason being is that *any* tune that you learned in the key of G (open strings, no capo) can be played in the key of A *without* having to learn a new set of notes, fingerings or positions.

Communicating the Correct Chords

One problematic caveat to this "nice and easy" transition from G to A (capo 2), is how you would describe the chords to a mandolinist (for example) who never uses a capo. You cannot say that the chords are "G, C and D7." Because, when capoed at the second fret, every chord name has to be moved forward one letter in the alphabet, just like you had to change the names of the open strings forward one letter, in order to properly read your tuner. Therefore the chord names change as follows:

G becomes A (not "H")
C becomes D
D7 becomes E7

And so, the three primary chords for "Cripple Creek" (or *any* tune) in the key of A, are A, D and E7. These chords are what the mandolinist plays. Your banjo chords are still perceived as G, C and D7 by you, but your capos have "automatically" transposed those chords to the key of A.

Confused? I don't blame you if you *are!* There is always more music theory to explore on such topics as this. Future explanations lie ahead (in this volume and the next) to help clear up the many questions that this whole "lecture" may have left with you.

The following pages contain three variations of "Cripple Creek," as well as new accompaniment ideas for the tune. For the initial melody, see Volume 1, page 72. If you don't have the capo and the other paraphernalia, feel free to go ahead and play it in G without the capo. If you have a capo along with the "equipment" to get the fifth string up to an A pitch, then try it in A/capo 2. You can always take a chance, and try "cranking" your fifth string peg from G to A, however "The Management" will not be held responsible for broken fifth strings! On the audio, I play the original version of "Cripple Creek" from Volume 1, in conjunction with these new versions. You will hear it both in G, and then again in A/capo 2.

Later on, there is a chapter devoted to a few tunes commonly capoed at the second fret to accommodate those mandolin and fiddle players (not to mention bassists!) you will be meeting up with at future bluegrass jam sessions.

Cripple Creek—Variations

Traditional—Arr. by Jeff Belding

Variation 3:

A G mid ind   C   G   (G)   D7   G

("9/10" position - Volume 1, page 37)

B G*   (G)   (lift)   (G)   D Barre 7**   G

** Barring - See
Vol. 1, page 37.

(Stop - Chords tacet until the final measure.)

Tag: G   ring   ind   pink   D7   G

TH I TH TH

* Even though G is the chord symbol, the use of the 9/10 position is a lick that "belongs" in the "G chord realm." The chord symbols aren't always to be taken literally by the banjo player. Sometimes, they just represent what the accompanist is playing for back-up.

Remember, the chords of G, C, and D7 are "perceived" chords for the capoed banjo. Having said that, a guitar player who also has a capo at the second fret, can use those "perceived" chords to accompany the banjo.

However, mandolinists, fiddlers and bass players are thinking in *actual* chords of A, D, and E (or E7).

CHAPTER 4

MUSIC THEORY LESSON: THE KEY OF G AND THE G MAJOR SCALE

Gaining a Greater Knowledge of Notes on the Banjo Neck Through an Understanding of How to Construct a G Major Scale

The G major scale that was first presented in Volume 1, page 31, is a good place to start for understanding the notes on the neck of your banjo. The notes found within the G scale are "building blocks" for melodies in the key of G. These same notes are also building blocks for various chords found in the key of G.

To take you on a (hopefully...) small tangent, say you want to be in the key of A. You would need to know the notes of the A major scale as a different set of building blocks. Fortunately for us banjo pickers, there is a shortcut to the key of A that doesn't cause "Theoretical Brain Freeze": If you know the chords, licks, and finger patterns in the key of G, just clamp your capo on the second fret and tune the fifth string, G, up higher to A. Now, all of the finger patterns you know without the capo (key of G), are *transposed* to the key of A.

Up until now, you may have been playing "Cripple Creek" with a guitar-playin' buddy in the key of G (*no* capo). But one day, in walks a fiddle player who says, "*I* play "Cripple Creek" in the key of A." Not to worry —just capo at the second fret, tune the fifth string up to A, and play "Cripple Creek" just as you know it, but now at this "two frets higher" position, and you and your new fiddler friend will get along just fine.

Back to the key of G and the G major scale.
Play the G scale in one octave from open G or third string to high G or fifth:

Example 1

Notice that the "letter name" of each individual note appears above the staff. The notes are also numbered *below* the staff from 1 to 8. You will find that notes 1 through 7 are each a different consecutive letter of the alphabet. Also, note number 8 is the same letter as note number 1.

Hopefully, by now you've memorized the letter names of the open strings! If so, you already have half of the note names in this scale memorized. They are: G, B, D and high G.

Name	G (3rd string, open)	B (2nd string, open)	D (1st string, open)	(High) G (5th string)
Number	#1	#3	#5	#8

So now, it's just a matter of filling in the spaces where the fretted notes belong. You are building the scale in this way so you can see the logic behind the G major scale and ultimately any major scale. Let us continue this process by posing two obvious questions:

1. What is George Washington's first name?

2. What is the name of the first note of The G major scale?

If you answered #1 "George" and #2 "G", then CONGRATULATIONS! You are on the way to a deeper understanding of the construction of the G scale without having to memorize each individual note.

Okay, here's the open string part of this scale:

Example 2

```
                                                                    High
Name: G (or 3rd)          B (or 2nd)          D (or 1st)            G (or 5th)
 T                            0                    0                     |
 A       0                                                              ▼
 B                                                                      0
Number: 1                    3                    5                     8
```

Now, you have to fill in the notes that you are probably not as sure of. If you know your alphabet from A through G (don't we all *?),* you will find this quite simple. Just be aware that there is one note (#2) between G and B, one note (#4) between B and D, and *two* notes (#'s 6 and 7) between D and high G.

Thus, start your G scale at G, and then—just write down the alphabet in order from A to G. The only caveat is that F is sharped (#):

"Given"   From here, it's just a matter of the alphabet!

|

G (open)   A   B   C   D   E   F#   G (high)

Now comes the time to answer that burning question: Why is F *sharped?* Here is a short answer:

The 7th and 8th note of *any* major scale *must* be one-half step apart from each other. That is to say, there is *no fret* that lies between those two final *highest* notes of a major scale. That may be hard to visualize, since in Example 1, the final two notes were on different strings. This time, put the 7th and 8th notes on the *same* string.

Example 3

```
                                                                    High
Name: G        A        B        C        D    E    F#             G (New Location!)
 T                                          0    2    4                  5
 A      0        2                          
 B                        0        1
Number: 1        2        3        4        5    6    7                  8
```

F# (7) and G (8) are right next to each other!

28

Notice that the location of note #8 (high G) is changed. It was shown previously as being on the fifth string, *open*. It is now shown at the first string, fifth fret. Both the fifth string open, and the first string, fifth fret are the *exact* same pitch of high G. Seeing this high G at the first string, fifth fret, helps illustrate the point that F sharp and high G are right next to each other fret-wise as they should be. Again, this one fret distance is a *half-step*. Playing the high G at the fifth string, open, is just an easier and more convenient way to get smoothly from the F sharp to the high G.

So far, the G scale has been discussed in terms of just *one* octave. In other words, you start at a low pitch G note, which is the lowest available G on the banjo. Then, you work your way up from there to the next highest G note, *one octave* above the G that you started on. Now, here's what the G scale looks like when going higher yet, beyond that one octave limit. You may not be quite ready to go another *full* octave, but a couple more additional notes can enhance your melody-playing possibilities:

Example 4

As you look at the last note of the second measure, you can see that the order of alphabetical notes you began on in measure one, start over again at the last note of measure two. You may also remember this A and B note as the "9/10" position (see Volume 1, page 37). It provided you with the range of notes you needed to play the two Irish jigs presented in Volume 1 (Pages 38/39 and 63).

Hopefully, it's becoming more clear at this point how those higher notes get their names. Now, you may well ask, "Why should I care about this? I just wanna play and not be worried about what notes I'm playing!" True, you can go through your life as a fine banjo player with*out* this kind of knowledge, but you *would* be missing out on the ability to gain new insights: how to find new chords, create new licks that are all your own, and perhaps even compose your own music!

Look at the final measure of Example 4. You have an F#, an E, and then open D or first string. This is followed by a pinch to end or "punctuate" the exercise. The scale did not return all the way down to the low G or third string at the end. This was done intentionally to illustrate another extension of the G scale. In this case, you will take your scale "backwards" to the available lower notes *below* the original starting note at the G or third string. This will take you back to your D or fourth string, open.

By now, you should be aware that your banjo has *two* D strings (at least when in G tuning): One is on the *first* string (the higher octave) and another is on the *fourth* string (the lower octave). Another informational take-away that you should place in your "mental notebook" are the names of the notes on the D or first string that have been presented so far:

• D, or *open* first string

• E, at the first string, 2nd fret, and

• F#, at the first string, 4th fret

So for now, you have a "given" of the location of D, E, and F# on your D or first string, and they are worth memorizing (remember, it's just the *alphabet,* D, E, and F#—save for the sharp sign).

Knowing this information, here's a new rule:

> Any note on the first string at *any* given fret, has its *matching* note name on the fourth string at the *same* given fret. Therefore, as go F#, E, and D (reverse order) on the *first* string, so goes F#, E, and D on the *fourth* string, same frets, one octave lower in pitch.

Using the last measure from Example 4 as a starting point, here is a new exercise based on those three all-important notes on your first and fourth strings. Get used to calling them by their actual letter names!

Example 5

| (← High →) | (Pinch) | (← Low →) | (Pinch) | (← High →) | (Pinch) | (← Low →) | (Pinch) |

```
        F#  E  D    D     F#  E  D    D     F#  E  D    D     F#  E  D    D
T  ┌┌:   4  2  0    0              0   4  2  0    0              0  ┐
A  ││   x  x  x    x    x  x  x  x    x  x  x  x    x  x  x  x  :│
B  └└         0            0   4  2  0            0   4  2  0     ┘
                     G            G            G            G
```

The next example incorporates *all* of the newly-identified notes in the G scale, extended up *higher* (in pitch) and then extended down *lower* (in pitch). It's a good idea to return any scale exercise to its starting note (a.k.a. the *Root* of the scale). In so doing, you will see how this exercise goes up, comes down, and then slightly up again to get you back "home" to the root note of G:

Example 6

```
                                    High---------------------------------
    G   A   B   C    D   E   F#  G    A   B   A   G    F#  E   D   C
                          0   2   4             9                4   2   0
T  ┌┌:              0   1                  10      10               1 ┐
A  ││  0  x  2  x    x   x   x   x    x   x   x   x    x   x   x   x┘
B  └└                  0              0
```

```
        Low--------------------------------------  Open  Low------------------  Open  Low  3-string
    B   A   G   F#   E   D   E   F#   G    F#  E   F#   G    D   Pinch
    0                                                              0
T  ┌                   4       2       4   0  x    x   x    0  x    x  0  x  R :┐
A  │   x  2  x  0  x   x    x   x   x   x      4  2  4      0     0        ┘
B  └                                                              0
```

The following example is yet another variation of "Cripple Creek," which is meant to give you some insight into how these G Scale notes can be used. You will notice it deviates quite a bit from the original melody, especially in the B part (rather than a repeat of B, there are two different versions of B!). You might say, "The better you know this-here G Scale, the more crazy stuff you can do for improvising on a tune in the key of G."

Example 7— "Cripple Creek": More variations making use of the G major scale notes.

All-important scale/melody notes are marked. The rest are "filler."

If the second version of the B part of the previous variation is a little too "bananas" for you right now, you can always repeat the first B part twice.

As you can see, using this G scale for improvisation isn't necessarily "clear-cut," up and down movement of the scale. The use of the F# was done sparingly, as that particular note is a little more "dangerous" when used against a G or C chord. Therefore, its usage was saved for the final measures of each section, since that's where the D7 chord comes into play, in which case F# works just fine.

That is not to say that F# can never be used against the G or C chords. Its usage just has to be more carefully planned. Ultimately, your ear will tell you if your choices of G scale notes are right or wrong.

And so ends your first Music Theory Lesson. As mentioned in the previous book, it can be a daunting subject. But realize, that every little bit of understanding that you take away from these music theory lessons will reap huge rewards for you, not to mention your future as both a banjo player and (more importantly) a musician.

CHAPTER 5

THIS STOP—MINOR CHORDS

Nothing sounds better on a banjo, than minor chords. Minor chords bring a dark, melancholy or sinister quality to traditional tunes like "The Cuckoo," "Little Sadie," "Shady Grove" and what could be more haunting than "Oh Death" as sung by Ralph Stanley?

What is the difference between a major chord and a minor chord? The technical answer is saved for a future music theory chapter (perhaps even for Volume 3). The simple answer to that question is that major chords sound "happy" and minor chords sound "sad."

Try strumming your A major barre chord (leaving out the fifth string) from "Home on the Range" (Volume 1, Page 53). Now compare by strumming A minor from "Irish Washerwoman" (Volume 1, Page 40). You can probably hear the stark difference between those two chords.

Four minor chords are presented in this chapter. You have seen the A minor (abbr. "min.") in use, if you have gone through Volume 1. The D minor, E minor, and F minor are presented here for the first time.

Page 33 makes use of the Amin, Dmin, and Emin. The chord progression moves through two measures each of:

Amin - Amin - Dmin - Dmin - Emin - Emin - Amin - Amin

This series of chords make up the structure of a piece that I call "A Minor Madness." To get you used to moving through these chord changes, it is first presented as an accompaniment through the chord progression. Notice this accompaniment picking makes use of specific string alternations. The same is true for the picking part (the melody) starting in measure 9. The F minor will be put to use later, but try the fingering and give it a few "plucks" to check out the sound. Notice that the fourth string is *not* used on this F minor fingering, since the four-finger version of F minor is quite the knuckle-buster! Here are your four sample minor chords in diagram form:

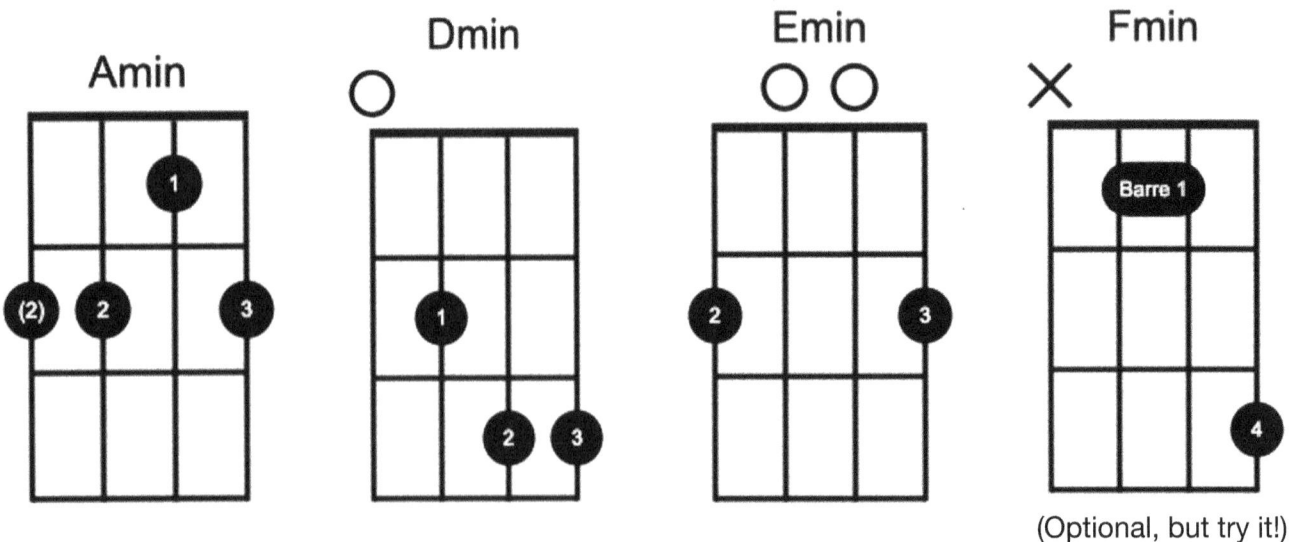

(Optional, but try it!)

"A Minor Madness"

The first section of this tune (measures 1–8) is an accompaniment for a guitar solo. Notice each section repeats two times. The next section starting at measure 9, is the first sample banjo solo, accompanied by guitar, also played twice. This interplay is presented in the banjo/guitar duets section of the audio.

This arrangement of guitar and banjo "switching off" continues with each variation of the piece. The banjo accompaniment is only shown at the very beginning, so be aware of the right time to switch to the "back-up" for the next guitar solo. Memorizing the accompaniment part would be a good idea for smoothness of operation to help get you through this tune.

Keep in mind that the chord structure written above the measures does *not* always mean that the banjo is literally holding down the chords at all times. Sometimes, part of the melody might "belong" with a chord, but doesn't necessarily fit within the chord fingering *verbatim*. Those differences are pointed out wherever possible.

A Minor Madness—Chord Structure

By Jeff Belding

Back-up: Amin — Move mid — (Amin) — Dmin — (Dmin)

TH   M   TH   M   (etc.)
 I   I

Emin — (Emin) — Amin — (Amin)

Solo: Amin — (Amin) — Dmin — (Dmin)

Emin — (Emin) — Amin — (Amin)

A Minor Madness—Variation 1

Amin (Single notes)　　(A*m) (Chord down)　　Dmin　　(Dm) (Single notes)

*min or m are *both* legitimate abbreviations for minor*

5　Emin　　(Em)　　(Single notes)　Amin (Single notes)　(Am) (Single notes)

9　Amin　　(Am)　　Dmin　　(Dm)

13　Emin　　(Em)　　Amin　　(Am)

For this next solo of "A Minor Madness" you will delve into moving "known chord fingerings" to different parts of the banjo neck. In Volume 1, it was discussed how barre chords that are moved to different parts of the neck have various different letter names (Volume 1, page 37). It was also briefly mentioned how the "fingering shape" of a D chord when moved up to higher-numbered frets, becomes a "new" type of G chord (Volume 1, bottom of page 65).

Consider the A minor chord which you know is at the first and second frets. If you move that "chord shape" further up the neck to frets 6 and 7, it becomes a *new* version of D minor. If you again, take that *same* fingering and move it up two more frets (8 and 9), you have a new version of E minor.

Now, take a look at the F minor chord fingering which you haven't used yet. In its original position, it's at frets 1 and 3. If you take that fingering, and move it up to frets 5 and 7, you have a *new* version of an A minor chord. Why this is the case, and how these various "movable chord shapes" get their names will be covered in future music theory discussions. In the meantime, take a look at your *new* A minor, D minor, and E minor chords in tablature form (Variation 2). They are presented here as both three-string "plucks," as well as separately picked strings while holding down these various fingerings.

34

A Minor Madness—Variation 2

"New" Amin from Fmin chord shape------------------------ "New" Dmin from Amin chord shape------------------------

```
T|--7----7----7----7----|--7-----5----5-----7---|--7----7----7----7----|--7----6----6-----7---|
A|--5--x--5--x--5--x--5--x--|-----5------------x--R--|--7--x--7--x--7--x--7--x--|-----6------7-----x--R--|
B|----------------------|-----------------------|--7----7----7----7----|----------------------|
```

M   M I TH I M
I
TH

"New" Emin from Amin chord shape------------------------ "New" Amin------------------------

```
5
T|--9----9----9----9----|--9-----8----8-----9---|--7----7----7----7----|--7----7----5-----7---|
A|--8--x--8--x--8--x--8--x--|-----8------------x--R--|--5--x--5--x--5--x--5--x--|-----5------5-----x--R--|
B|--9----9----9----9----|-----9-----------------|--5----5----5----5----|----------------------|
```

A Minor Madness—Variation 3

Mixing the *new* minor chords with the *original* minor chords:

Amin (New---)   Dmin (New---)

```
T|-----5----7----7------7---|-----7----7------7---|-----7----7------7---|-----7----7------7---|
A|--5---------5----5--------|--5---------5----5--------|--6---------6----6--------|--6---------6----6--------|
B|--5--------------------0--|--0------------------0--|--7---------7----7--------|--7---------7----7--------|
```

Emin (New---)   Amin (New-------------) Amin (Original----------)

```
5
T|-----9----9------9---|-----9----9------9---|-----7----7---|-----2----2---|
A|--8---------8----8--------|--8---------8----8--------|--5---------5--x--|--1---------1--x--|
B|--9---------9----9--------|--0------------------9--x--|--5--------------|--2---------2--x--|
```

Amin (Single notes) Amin (New-------------) Dmin (Original----------) Dmin (New-------------)

```
9
T|-----0----2------1---|-----7----7------7---|-----3----3------3---|-----7----7------7---|
A|--2--x------x--1---x--|--5---------5----5--x--|--3---------3------3--|--6---------6------6--|
B|-----------------0--|--0------------------0--|--2---------2----2--x--|--7---------7----7--x--|
```

Emin (New----------------------- Add   Lift)   Am (New) Am (Original--------------------)
                                  pink pink

```
13
T|-----9----9------9---|-----10----9---|-----7----7------2---|-----2---|
A|--8---------8----8--------|--8---------9--x--|--5---------1------1--|--1---------2--x--|
B|--9---------9----9--------|--0------------------0--|--0---------0--------|--2--x--x--x--2--x--|
```

A Minor Madness—Variation 4

Amin (New--)   Dmin (New--)

Emin (New--)   Amin (New--)

(Amin)
(Single notes) Am (original)   Am (New-------------)   Dmin (New------------------)   Dmin (original---------)
ind   ring   mid

Emin (original--)   (Amin)
(Single notes)   Amin
ring   Lift   ring   mid   ring   ring   ring   mid   mid

"Reverse Mountain Curve"—Combining Minor and Major Chords

Coming up, you have a banjo instrumental called "Reverse Mountain Curve." The E minor chord and the G (major) chord are used together in all kinds of tunes, be they folk, classical or bluegrass. Here is a "roadmap" for the chord progression of the tune:

Emin	Emin	G	G
Emin	Emin	G	G
Emin	Emin	Amin	Amin
D7	D7	G	G

Each chord shown represents one full measure of four beats in a time signature of "4/4 time." (See Volume 1, Page 51 for some more explanation of time signatures.)

Notice the use of the A minor chord on the third line of this chord progression (see Volume 1, Page 48, bottom text for more on "Chord Progressions"). Now explore "Reverse Mountain Curve," starting with the chord accompaniment (*a.k.a.* "Back-up").

Reverse Mountain Curve—Chord Structure

Reverse Mountain Curve—First Solo

By Jeff Belding

(To Back-up)

* Measures 7 and 15: Variation on a common lick from
Volume 1 (Page 44, #5), now with the addition of the
third string pull-off on the *seventh* 8th note beat of the
measure.

In order to be ready for playing Solo #2 of "Reverse Mountain Curve," you will need to try some exercises involving new maneuvers for your fretting hand. The picking hand still abides by the standard picking hand rules (see page 8). These following examples are a "sneak-peek" into the world of what is known as "Melodic Banjo."

Preparatory Exercises for
Reverse Mountain Curve, Solo #2

1 E minor scale "fragment" - First four notes of the E minor scale

2 First *five* notes of the E minor scale

3 Two measures of E minor - Two measures of A minor

Am - Short form

4 Two measures of E minor - Two measures of G

Solo #2 of this tune is 32 measures long, whereas Solo #1 was 16 measures repeated twice. The first 16 measures of Solo #2 are more straight-forward, and then the final 16 measures are where your knowledge of these exercises are put to the test. May The Force be with you!

Reverse Mountain Curve—Solo #2

By Jeff Belding

C H A P T E R 6

INTRODUCING THE F CHORD

The Three-Finger F Chord:

Tab Form: Diagram Form:

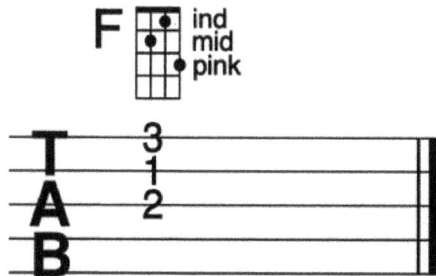

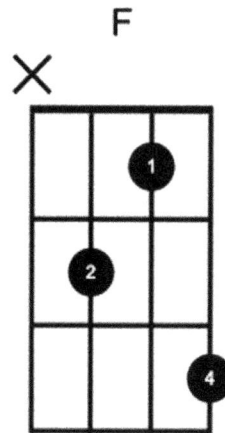

In this chapter, you will explore two traditional tunes that make use of the F chord:

"Old Joe Clark"

and

"Yonder Stands Little Maggie"

First, you will learn "Old Joe Clark" in the key of G without the use of a capo. But ultimately, you want to be able to play it in the key of A, using the capo at the second fret like you did with "Cripple Creek."

"Yonder Stands Little Maggie" is almost always played in the key of G, so no capo is necessary on that one. You will also use this tune as a springboard for a different kind of accompaniment that is used often in the world of bluegrass jamming.

Notice from the diagram that this particular F chord (there are *plenty* of others!) is a three-finger version. The four-finger version of F is difficult to manipulate, so you can work up to that version at a later date. Notice, too, the use of the pinky on the first string. It makes the reach to the third fret easier to manage, and it will prepare you for that all-challenging four-finger F to come.

Here's a basic melody to "Old Joe Clark." Again, *no* capo for now.

Old Joe Clark—EZ Melody

Traditional—Arr. Jeff Belding

* The chords above the staff are there for the sake of the accompaniment.

Any chords in italics are actual *held down* banjo chords.

Old Joe Clark—Basic Back-up

This simple accompaniment is provided to get you used to the chord stucture of "Old Joe."
Notice how the F chord is handled in measure 12.

On the next page, you will find a more challenging and interesting back-up part for this tune.

Old Joe Clark—Fancier Back-up

You can either use this or the previous back-up part for other people's solos.
They are both effective. Work with the version that you're most comfortable with for now.

Once again, this friendly reminder bears repeating: When playing back-up, "Shhhhhhh."

And next, submitted for your approval, you have a variation on the melody to "Old Joe."

Old Joe Clark—Variation on the Melody

On this version of the tune, you will find a lot more eighth notes, as well as sixteenth note slides and hammer-ons.

If you find it hard to grasp, go back to the original melody to better absorb it into your brain. Also remember, in a jam situation, it may be best to play the original melody when initially trying it out—especially if some over-zealous guitarist kicks it off at 250 BPM *!!!

* BPM—Beats per minute

On the audio, you will hear the two versions of "Old Joe" with banjo back-ups in between: Once without the capo (Key of G) and again later, with capo at second fret (Key of A).

Moving the F Chord Shape to Get a New Version of a G Chord

You have now been through "Old Joe Clark," in both its melody and accompaniment aspects. Having worked with that, you should be well versed in the location and fingering of the F chord as well as getting comfortable with its usage in a tune. You have seen that both the barre chord and the (regular) D chord shapes can be moved around the banjo neck to give these chord shapes different names in their other locations.

Just to review some examples:

Barre 2nd fret, "A"
Barre 5th fret, a new version of "C"
Barre 7th fret, a new version of "D"

D shape moved up to 7th, 8th and 9th frets, a new version of "G"

Once again, you ask,"Why is this? Where do these names come from?" The answer lies ahead, but you will have to wait until Volume 3 for the explanation.

Now, how about your new F chord shape? Like the two chord shapes previously mentioned, this one is also a movable-finger shape whose name is based on its fretted location. The F chord as you learned it, is at frets 1, 2, and 3. If you take that finger shape, and shift it up to fret numbers 3, 4, and 5, you come to a new version of a "G" chord (G being the letter after F).

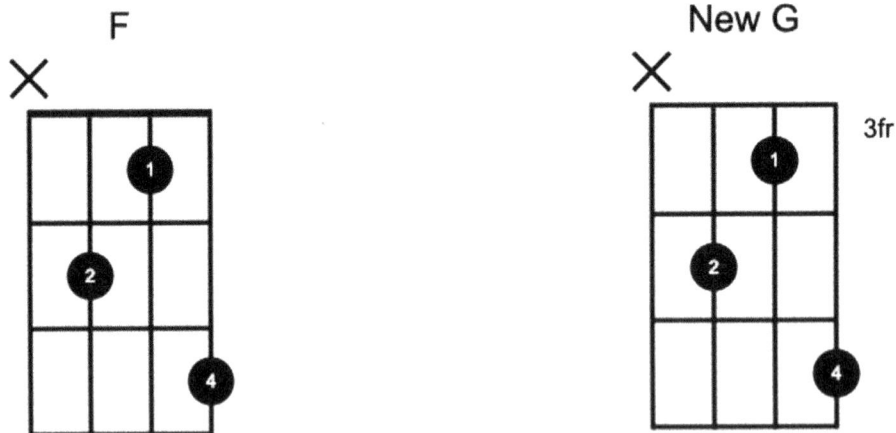

To get you used to moving from F to (new) G and back again, the following are some exercises for you to play moving this F chord shape back and forth. This leads up to a *new* type of banjo back-up for the old traditional tune,"Yonder Stands Little Maggie." Accompaniments of this kind use a short, "clipped" chord, that is "hit" on the second and fourth beats of a measure. It is a very effective form of back-up on banjo, often heard in a bluegrass band setting.

These exercises are followed by three solos for the tune.

So, now explore "Yonder Stands Little Maggie."

Moving the F Chord Shape Two Frets Higher:
Thus Forming a "New" G Chord

Ex. 1   F   (+ 2 Frets) G (New - from "F shape")   F   G (New)

M
I
TH

Ex. 2: Some forward-backward rolls: The pauses are there to give you some time to make your move.

G (New)   F   G   D
mid ind pink   mid ind pink   ind mid   ind mid pink

Yonder Stands Little Maggie
Banjo Accompaniment

"Chops" on Beats 2 and 4

G (New--)   F---

Beats: (1)   2   (3)   4
(Rest)   (Rest)

M
I
TH

G (New----------------)   D--------------------   G (New---)

47

Yonder Stands Little Maggie—3 Banjo Solos

Traditional—Arr. by Jeff Belding

(For more on index picking 3rd string,
see up and coming Chapter 7.)

(To Back-up)

(To Back-up)

(To Back-up)

For an ending, you can use the same one from "Old Joe Clark" (Page 45).

INDEX STEALS THIRD

In Chapter 6, you played a solo for "Yonder Stands Little Maggie," where your picking hand index finger (I) came "inside" to the third string. Your index finger's usual assignment is to pick the second string. However, as picking patterns become more complex, it becomes necessary for that index finger to "move over" to do some work on the third string. There will even come a day when your index goes even *further* to the *fourth* string but that is for another time and another book.

The basic rule for the necessity of your index to "come hither" to your third string is as follows:

Whenever the thumb (TH) of the picking hand picks the fifth string, and the very next *8th* note is the third string, then your index finger (I) *must* pick that third string for smoothness of operation.

If this *didn't* happen, the thumb would have to "jump over" the fourth string to get to that up-and-coming third string. This is actually possible at slow-to-moderate tempos, but once you get to 180 BPM or beyond, it is just too awkward of a movement to execute. Therefore, you have an entire chapter devoted to this maneuver to get you in the habit of doing it correctly from the *start*.

You begin with ten exercises that give your index finger one heck of a workout. In some of these exercises, you will also find it necessary to use your index after the thumb picks a *fourth* string eighth note as well. Using "thumb to thumb" is fine for two quarter notes, but it just doesn't work well for two consecutive eighth notes.

You will also be working up to a *new* G fill that should be a part of *every* banjo player's repertoire of licks. After that, you will be presented with two tunes of mine ("Stealing Third" and "Busy Pointer"). So, start doing sit-ups with your index finger, and let's get *BUSY!*

Jammin' with "The Spouses"
(Pete and Kim Conklin and Edwina and Jeff Belding

Index on 3rd String—Exercises

Repeat each exercise 8X (For more on this concept, see Volume 1, Pages 44 and 67)

1

Pick w/ index!

2

3

4 Adding some fretted notes:

5

(Continues)

More Index on 3rd String:

C and D Chord Licks

Repeat each exercise 8X

6 C (Hold down C chord throughout)

Be *very* mindful when you see picking hand fingerings suddenly showing up! These are the "Danger Zones" where the correct picking finger usage is *essential!*

7 D Licks

Hold down w/ ind throughout

D

TH I   I   I TH   M I TH   TH I   I   I TH   M
                                                                          TH

8 C (Hold down C chord throughout)

M I TH   TH I   M I TH

9 More D Licks

Hold down throughout

ring ind   ind ring   Add mid   Lift ring   ring ind   D

TH I   I TH   TH M I TH I   TH I   I TH

10 "Combo Platter"

G   C   D Lick   G

                              ring ind

M I TH   TH I M I TH   TH I   I TH

Building a New G Fill:

Using Your Newly-Aquired Index Finger Skills

1 Becoming aware of the Picking Hand Index (I) finger's "responsibilities":

Add mid   Add mid

TH TH I   I TH M   TH I   I TH   TH I   I TH   TH I   I TH

2 Adding more fretted notes and a slide into the mix:

mid   Move mid   mid   Move mid   mid mid   Move mid   mid mid   Move mid

TH I   I TH   TH I   I TH   TH TH I – (sl) I TH   TH I – (sl) I TH

3 The biggest challenge: Adding an extra plucked note at the end of a slide—It's a KILLER!

First, slowly: Pick with M   Now, quicker: Pick with M   Pick with M   Adding a "Prefix"   Pick with M   Pick with M

TH   I —— (sl)   TH I – (sl) TH I – (sl)   TH TH I —(sl)   TH TH I —(sl)

These two notes must sound *simultaneously!* (Go to the audio to check out the sound.)

4 The Full G Fill #2—An essential part of your library of banjo licks:

mid   Move mid   mid   Move mid   mid   Move mid

TH TH I – (sl) I TH M   I – (sl) I TH   I – (sl) I TH   TH TH M I TH

"Stealing 3rd" With Index Finger

Here is a tune that puts many of your Index finger skills to the test.

By Jeff Belding

Busy Pointer

Here's another "Pickin' Party" for your Pointer Finger!

Remember: When you see picking hand markings, they must be followed *exactly* as written!

By Jeff Belding

BUILDING A BANJO SOLO—"RED WING"

How do you construct a banjo solo? There are steps to be taken to bring a song from its basic melody into a full-blown appealing and pleasing banjo solo.

The banjo is somewhat of an exotic animal of the instrument world. For one thing, it's usually tuned to an open-string G chord. Also, because of G tuning, it has this strange characteristic of the highest-pitched string being on the "wrong" side of the string alignment. When in G tuning, that highest-pitched string is a G note.

The Drone String—Sometimes An Asset, Sometimes a Liability

That high G, which is "ever-present" and sometimes hard to even avoid, is also known as a "drone string." Its function (other than being part of a G chord and C chord) is to provide some "coloration" to other common banjo chords.

When that high G string is used with an A chord, it adds the harmony of A7. When used with a D chord, it hints at being a "D sus 4." When used strategically, it becomes an asset to the chord harmony, but it can also create some unpleasant dissonance when used with a chord that is "less friendly" like an F sharp.

The music theory behind these aforementioned chord names is not crucial at this juncture in your learning curve. Your ear will tell you easily enough if that high G string is working with or against the chord at hand. When playing a banjo roll within a particular chord, sometimes you have to decide if that high G is working or if it is best to avoid it somehow by changing up the picking hand pattern.

A Guide To Get You Started On Your Own Banjo Arrangements

The drone string is just one of the challenges you are up against when creating a banjo solo from a basic melody. Banjo rolls themselves have a way of stretching and changing the typical timing of the way a basic melody might be sung. Now that you've been given fair warning of the problems in assembling a banjo solo from a known melody, the following are six steps you can use to come up with that elusive arrangement of a popular tune on your banjo:

1. **Learn the melody in a basic form (mainly, quarter notes and half notes).**

2. **Write down the chord structure for the song**—This way, you become aware of how many measures each chord lasts for and if there are measures that contain two or more chords. See the bottom of page 36 for a shorthand version of a chord chart (in that case for "Reverse Mountain Curve").

3. **Learn to *play* the chord structure**—You can do this by either using your basic accompaniment patterns or just strumming in quarter note down strums. Once you're comfortable with *this,* try humming or singing the tune as you play through the chords.

4. **Create "Variation 1"**—This is where your solo will begin to take shape as an arrangement. Add some "filler notes" to your basic melody in places where there are longer pauses. Use notes that are part of the chord in that particular section or measure. Each filler note would be on a different string, as if you are playing all or part of a banjo roll or fill (e.g. G Fill #2 from Chapter 7).

5. **Play through the basic melody, immediately followed by your newly-constructed Variation 1**
Even better, make a recording of this mini arrangement. Upon playing back your recording, listen for the differences as well as the similarities between the two versions.

6. **Create "Variation 2"**
Your second variation should be busier and more ornate than the first one. This can be done by adding more 16th note hammer-ons and pull-offs, and stretching or syncopating the melody. You can also leave out portions of the melody altogether. These parts of the "missing melody" can be replaced by a banjo roll on a chord that "sounds more interesting" than playing the melody verbatim.

Now, here are these steps as you build an arrangement of "Red Wing."

Red Wing—Basic Version

Step One: Learning the Basic Melody

Traditional—Arr. by Jeff Belding

```
      C                    ( C )                    G                    G
17    mid                        pink  pink  mid
T--2-------2-----0-----2-----5-----4-----2-----0-----------------0-----0-----2-----0-----
A-------x---R----x-----x-----x-----x-----x-----x-----x--R----0----x--R----R-----x-----x-----x--
B----------------------------------------------------------------------------------------
```

```
      D                    ( D )                    G                    ( G )  pink  pink  ring
21
T--0-------------------------0-----2-----0-----0-----------------0-----5-----4-----3-----
A-------x--R----2--x--R----R-----x-----x-----x-----x--R----0----x--R----R-----x-----x-----x--
B----------------------------------------------------------------------------------------
```

```
      C                    ( C )                    G                    ( G )
25
T--2-------2-----0-----2-----------4-----2-----0-----------------0-----0-----2-----0-----
A-------x--R----x-----x-----x-----x-----x-----x-----x--R----0----x--R----R-----x-----x-----x--
B------------------------------0-----------------------------------------------------------
```

```
      D                    ( D )                    G                    ( G )  (Pick-ups to Variation 1)
29
T--0-------------------------1-----0-----------------------------------------------------
A-------x--R----2--x--R----R-----x-----x--2--x----0--x--R----R----R----R-----x-----x-----x--
B--------------------------------------------------------------0-----2-----4--------------
```

Step Two—Write down the chord structure for the song. As you can see, this has been taken care of in our previous example. Watch out for any measure that contains two chords, in this case, measure 15.

Step Three—Learn to play the chord structure. Be able to hum the melody and play the chords above the melody using your knowledge of accompaniment. The best way to handle the A chord, is a *full* barre across the second fret (all four available strings).

A - Full barre

←Barre 2nd fret with Index

One measure of the A chord back-up (measure 7) would look like this:

```
T-----------2--------2------
A--2---x-----x---x-----x----
B------------2---------------
```

Your "half and half" measure (15) would look like this:

```
      A           D
T-----------2--------4------
A--2---x-----x---x----3-----
B------------0---------------
```

On the audio, you will hear my rendition of "chords and hum" for the "Red Wing" basic melody.

Red Wing—Variation 1

Step Four: Create Variation 1—Add Filler Notes

Arranged by Jeff Belding

Accent marks (>) show where the melody notes are "embedded" around the filler notes.

The pick-up notes are at the end of the basic melody.

* In the Key of G, D and D7
  are interchangeable.

(Continues)

* When a melody note falls on a "weak" or "unusual" beat, it is known as *Syncopation*.

(Pick-ups to Variation 2)

Step Five: Go back and play each version of "Red Wing" in succession. Record yourself, listen back and compare the two versions.

Red Wing—Variation 2

Step Six: Create Variation 2

Arranged by Jeff Belding

Variation 2 adds even more filler notes, more "frills," and sometimes veers away from the melody altogether!

G   (G)   C ("Melodic Lick")   G

TH I   TH I ← 👓
(Index picks 3rd!)   Be alert!

D7   G   A (barre)   D

TH I   TH I

G   (G)   C ("Melodic Lick")   G

TH I   TH I

D7   G   A (barre)   D7   G

TH I   TH I

C   C ("Melodic Lick")   G   (G)

D7   D (Hold D chord-------------)   G ("Melodic Lick")   (G)

(Continues)

25 C   C (Arpeggio*)   G   G (Arpeggio)

D (Lick)   D (Lick)   G Fill #2 (M)   G

Ending:
G (Back-up Tacet)   C   D (D chord down)   Strum Strum   D   G

(This ending was "lifted" from Volume 1, Page 27.)

* An *Arpeggio* (measures 26 and 28) is taking the notes
of a chord, and playing them one after the other,
rather than strumming or plucking them simultaneously.

For example, playing a forward/backward roll
on an open G chord is one form of a G arpeggio.

On the audio, you will find a recording with banjo/guitar interplay of all the versions of "Red Wing"
that were covered in this chapter. This will give you the opportunity to try both melody and back-up parts.
You will get a more detailed description of the arrangement on the audio itself.

CHAPTER 9

WALTZES

Playing waltzes on your banjo should become part of your regular repertoire of tunes. You should also have some basic knowledge of how to accompany someone playing or singing a waltz.

Refer to Volume 1, Pages 51 through 53 for some explanation on how waltzes work, as well as some tips on accompaniment in 3/4 (three-quarter) time. Unfortunately, it's a 4/4 time-biased world (at least in the U.S.A.), so "getting in the groove" of a waltz can be challenging, just from a lack of their everyday usage in typical bluegrass jams.

To prime you up for this waltz chapter, chant:

1 2 3 **1** 2 3 **1** 2 3 **1** 2 3

Well done! You just chanted four measures in waltz (three-quarter) time. Notice that the "1's" are in a larger font size, to help you see and hear how the natural accent of a waltz *is* on the first beat of each measure.

In bluegrass rhythm (or back-up) playing, 4/4 (four-quarter) time is often described in a rhythmic chant as—"Boom - chick - Boom - chick" for each measure of four beats.

On the other hand, the typical back-up chant for 3/4 (waltz time) is—"Boom - chick - chick" for each measure. "Home on the Range" found in Volume 1 on Page 53 is an example of waltz accompaniment.

The first featured waltzes in this chapter are in the key of C. Try the following waltz exercise using the primary chords in the key of C (C, F, and G):

Now, let's play some waltzes...

Woodland Waltz

By Jeff Belding

The Beautiful Blue Danube Waltz

(Theme #1)

Johann Strauss Jr. (Arr. Belding)

The Ash Grove Waltz

3/4
Time

Traditional—Arr. by Jeff Belding

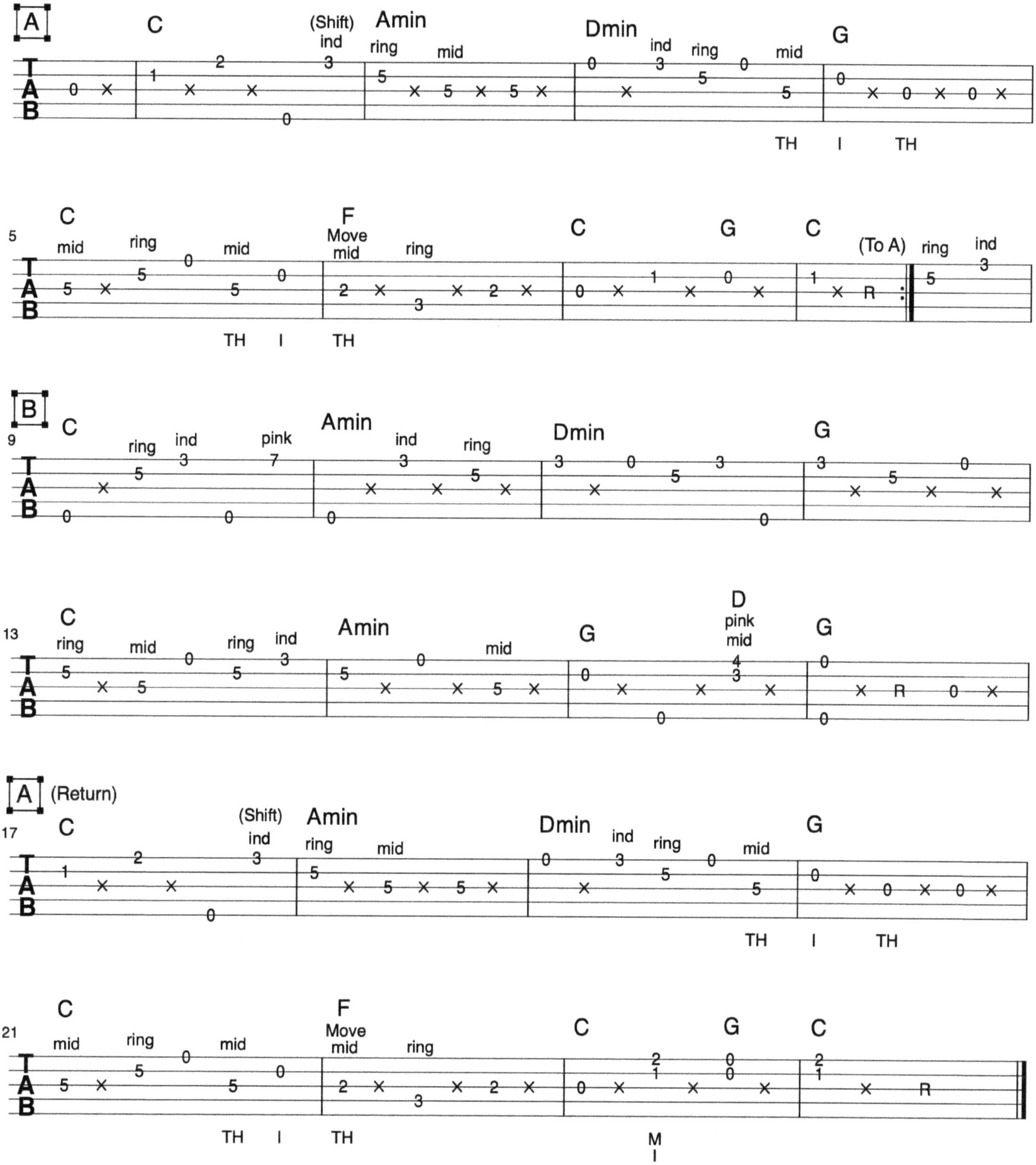

All the Good Times

Basic Version and Back-up

Key of G

Traditional—Arr. by Jeff Belding

All the Good Times

Variation 1 and More Back-up Ideas

Arranged by Jeff Belding

All the Good Times

Variation 2—More embellishments and more liberties taken with the melody

Arranged by Jeff Belding

* 12th Fret Harmonics: Lay the index finger lightly touching the 1st and 2nd strings at the12th fret (*Not* pressing down). The finger must be directly over the 12th fret "wire" rather than (the usual) between the fret "wires."

If the harmonics prove to be too difficult at first, you can still use a "regular" barre at the 12th fret on those two strings.

C H A P T E R 10

MORE CAPO 2 TUNES

Back in Chapter 3, you were presented with the idea of incorporating a capo into your arsenal of banjo equipment. As time goes on, you will find that your confidence level to "handle" yourself in bluegrass jam situations will grow, along with your ability level. When someone asks you if you would like to present a tune, you may find yourself accepting the offer more readily, rather than just passing it on to the next guy or gal.

Give the Mandolins and Fiddles Their Due

When it comes to fiddle tunes or instrumentals in general, you will want to be aware of the *keys* in which you play your various repertoire of tunes. If you learned something in the key of G (no capo involved), you have to be careful of the fact that a mandolinist or fiddle player may be used to playing that same tune in the key of A. It's always good "jam etiquette" to ask what key the fiddle player or mandolinist "likes the tune to be in."

If they do say, "key of A," then it's time to put your capo on the second fret, and go through all the steps that were covered in Chapter 3. Even better, it is best to have practiced these tunes at home with your capo *on,* in order to get used to what the fretboard looks like when capoed to A, while playing your "G-like" maneuvers.

Banjo Capo 2 Repertoire—A Partial List of Tunes

Of course you don't always have a way of knowing what the "most popular key" is for every tune on the planet. But here is a partial list of popular bluegrass instrumentals that are most commonly played in the key of A by fiddle and mandolin players, and therefore should be part of your "capo 2 (second fret) repertoire."

"Big Sandy"
"Bile Dem Cabbage Down"
"Bill Cheathem"
"Cherokee Shuffle"
"Cripple Creek"
"Devil's Dream"
"Old Joe Clark"
"Red Haired Boy"

You have already covered "Cripple Creek" and "Old Joe Clark," so it would behoove you to practice those tunes with the capo at the second fret. Not all of these tunes made it into this book but for now you can take on "Bile Dem Cabbage Down" and "Devil's Dream." The Tabs "look like" they are in G, but with your capo on, they are "automatically" transposed to A, which will make all of your 'fiddling friends' very happy. Okay, capos on, and get on with it…

Bile Dem Cabbage Down—Version 1 and Back-up

This tune has just one 8-measure progression that repeats over and over. Each soloist
would play that progression twice through, before passing it on to the next soloist.

Capo 2 for Key of A

Traditonal—Arr. by Jeff Belding

A special picking hand pattern that many
banjoists prefer. Not required, but *try* it!

Back-up—Played twice to accomodate the soloist.

(Repeat Back-up)

Bile Dem Cabbage Down—Variation 1

Capo 2 for Key of A

Arranged by Jeff Belding

Bile Dem Cabbage Down—Variation 2

Capo 2 for Key of A

Arranged by Jeff Belding

The Metronome And Its Use

Some of you may be old enough to remember the "classic" look of the metronome—a wooden box with a weighted pendulum, sitting on top of a piano. Those days are gone, as most are electronic, and you can easily get one as an app on your phone.

Metronomes, like electronic tuners, are of no help to you unless you use them properly. Complicating the issue further, the metronome (a machine) keeps perfect (metronomic) time, and the poor human being who is trying to play along with it does *not!*

Metronomes come with a speed adjustment, usually from 40 to 250. These numbers represent beats (or "clicks") per minute (abbreviated BPM). For example, "60 BPM" clicks along at the same speed as your watch's second hand (there I go, dating myself talking about a watch with hands!).

If you've never practiced with one of these devices before, here are some suggestions:

- Set your metronome at 60 BPM.
- With your middle finger picking just the first string over and over, try to play along with each click.
- You may find that you *really* have to hold back to stay with the clicks, so as not to "rush ahead."
- These beats are your *quarter notes.* If it helps, try counting "1-2-3-4-" over and over as you play along.

If this is going well for you, try this next step which is more challenging:

- With your device still set on 60, fit *two* of those first-string notes in the space of a single click.
- In this case, you are now picking *twice as fast* on that first string with your middle finger. These two notes per beat are your *eighth notes.*
- To play these eighth notes in as perfect time as possible, you must count out loud, "1 and 2 and 3 and 4 and," over and over.
- If at first you can't play and count, try just counting this out loud as your metronome clicks along.

The next step is to try an exercise that *alternates* four beats of eighth notes with four beats of quarter notes. You will find further explanation of this on the audio companion, since hearing how this works will help you even more. If you own a copy of Volume 1, you can find out more about these concepts on pages 13 and 15.

Now, try using the metronome with "77 Banjo Rolls" back in Chapter 1, page 12. You may have to set your metronome even lower to 40 BPM the first time you try any of these rolls, which for the most part (but not always) are in eighth notes. Rolls 1 and 2 should be very familiar to you by now. Therefore, it's more a matter of keeping up with "Mr. Machine," with your (soon to be) perfectly-timed eighth notes, and not having to worry about strings or picking hand fingers so much.

The metronome is the perfect tool for working on your "picking speed." For instance, you can work Roll #2 up to 60 BPM on a given day. Keep a record of that, then at your next practice start at 60 and see if you can work your way up to 80. Mark your progress as you increase your speed. Remember, playing something more slowly and *accurately* is more important than playing fast and carelessly. Continue this drill everyday, and the day may come when you will be able to roll along at 250 BPM, or *beyond.* At first try this for 10 minutes a day. Then go on practicing without the metronome...after all, it's a sanity thing, ya know!

Devil's Dream—Melody

Capo 2 for Key of A

Traditional—Arr. by Jeff Belding

* Taters are tempo setting "count off" licks.
To sound them out, say, "One Potater G, Pinch,
Two potater G, Pinch," etc. until you get to four.

Devil's Dream—Back-up and Variation

Capo 2 for Key of A

Arranged by Jeff Belding

Back-up—Play 4X total for soloist.

"Soldier's Joy"—Another Tune for Capo 2

The following rendition of "Soldier's Joy" involves the three primary chords in the key of C (C, F and G), with one little wrinkle. Fiddle players prefer to play it in the key of D. This is another common key for banjo players putting their capos on the second fret.

Some Info To Help You Understand Transposition

Think back to how you transposed tunes that were originally in the key of G (*no* capo), up to the key of A, with the capo placed on the second fret. The letter G is the "end" of the seven-letter "musical alphabet" (A - B - C - D - E - F - G). The questions that might follow are, "What happens after the letter G when going on from *there*? Is it H?" The answer is "No, it is A again." The musical alphabet is a continuum from one octave to the next: A - B - C - D - E - F - G - A - B, etc. See the Glossary for more details on the musical alphabet.

Therefore, your "perceived" primary chords for the key of *G* at capo 2 (G, C, and D), become actual named chords of A, D, and E. Each of those actual chords are the next alphabetical letter after their original *un*-capoed names.

Regarding your three "perceived" primary chords in the key of C (once again, C, F, and G): once your capo is in place, they must now change each of their names to the *next* letter in the alphabet. What do you think are their *actual* names in the newly capoed key of D? (Answer below*).

If you still don't have a capo available, go ahead and learn "Soldier's Joy" without it. Once you put the capo on, your fret markers may deceive you at first, but it's a fairly easy adjustment to this "new territory."

* Answer: D, G and A.

Soldier's Joy—Key of C (When un-capoed)

Capo 2 for Key of D

Traditional—Arr. by Jeff Belding

Situation Jeff

Jeff playing Gordie Acri's banjo bass,
Blythe, CA

Vito and Jeff pickin' at the Red Rooster Cafe,
New Paltz, NY

A trip on the Starship Enterprise to help me get
inspiration for Volume 3

"TURKEY IN THE STRAW"—ONE STEP AT A TIME...

Now, time to return to the key of G (*no* capo) and get started on a fiddle tune classic. There are many banjo renditions of this "Golden Turkey," but there's always room for one more!

The "Basic Turkey"—A Safe Bet When Speed Is of The Essence

The first (basic) rendition, starts with a simple "skeleton-like" version of the melody. Simple renditions like this one are good to keep in your back pocket, especially if some crazed fiddle player kicks it off at lightning speed! It may be your only hope to keep up with the furious pace at which this tune is often played!

The basic version is followed by a suggested back-up to get you used to the chord structure. Following that, you have Variation 1 with, of course, some more notes added to that basic version.

Variation 1—More of the Melodic Style

Variation 1 provides some more ground work for what is known as *melodic style* banjo playing. You've seen bits and pieces of melodic style licks in previous chapters, such as Chapter 5 on minor chords ("Reverse Mountain Curve"), and more recent chapters.

The gist of playing melodic style, is to play each consecutive note of a phrase on a different string, picked each time with a different picking-hand finger. Fretted notes often alternate with open strings or vice-versa. No hammer-ons or pull-offs are involved. The effect is that of very smooth-running, *legato* (full length to each note) passages.

It Ain't Easy—Take Your Time—It's a Very Gradual Process...

As mentioned, this melodic style works best in situations where many open strings are involved, which gives you the right set-up for melodic-style licks. It is also a very precise and demanding style, in that one mistake in the note "line-up" can throw you off a cliff. That is why you'll be introduced to the melodic style in as small doses as possible, thus, getting your feet wet gradually.

Variation 1 is followed by a variation on the accompaniment, just to give you some more appealing stuff to do with the chord progression. Then, there is a final Variation 2. The B part of this variation puts the melody in the "next higher octave," so prepare yourself for counting up to some higher frets, as high as 17!

The whole thing is punctuated with a fancy, melodic-style ending, and you now have plenty of ammunition to play the tune in a jam situation.

And now, "Turkey in the Straw," one step at a time...

Turkey in the Straw—Basic Melody and Back-up

Traditional—Arr. by Jeff Belding

(To Variation 1)

Turkey in the Straw—Var. 1 and Enhanced Back-up

Pick-ups are at the end of the previous back-up section.

Arranged by Jeff Belding

(To Variation 2)

Turkey in the Straw—Variation 2 and Ending

Arranged by Jeff Belding

Chords are not written above the Tab staff to avoid confusion. Accompanist can get the chords from the previous variation.

(No repeat of A)

B Octave higher—To the stratosphere!

CHAPTER 12

THE TAKE-AWAY AND THE LOOK AHEAD

The Take-Away

In Volume 1 of this banjo series, you were taken from the humble beginnings of starting your learning process, to an understanding of some of the important elements of making "banjoistic-sounding" banjo music. If Volume 1 "did its job," it made you a knowledgable-enough banjo player to sit in on some easy-going jam sessions.

The purpose of Volume 2 was to take your technical abilities gained from the first book and expand on them through increasing your repertoire of banjo tunes, teaching you a bunch of new chords, as well as giving you some insight into the Music Theory behind what you have learned to play.

The Look Ahead

In up and coming Volume 3, you can expect an even greater emphasis on Music Theory, with explanations that dig more deeply into such subjects as scales, chord construction, and tutorials to give you a greater understanding of chord progressions in various keys. Also, in Volumes 1 and 2, you have adhered strictly to G tuning (even when the capo was in use). In Volume 3, you will explore other fairly common banjo tunings.

A Library Of Licks For Your Mind's "File Cabinet"

A term that has come up often in this book, and is the subject of endless discussion in banjo circles, is the word "licks." You might recall many instances where a measure may have been labeled as a "D Lick" to give just one example. Take these licks and catalog them in a "mental portfolio." Be able to call them up when a particular chord in a measure of a song needs to be filled in with notes that belong with that chord.

So, how do you practice this sort of nebulous idea of calling up "the right lick, at the right time, for the right chord"? Most of the songs that you come across in bluegrass jamming situations will contain a G, C, and D (or D7) chord, but nothing more. Go back to the sample chord progression found in Volume 1, at the top of page 49. This is the progression in a nutshell (each chord being one full measure of 4 beats):

[:   G   G   C   C   D (7)   D (7)   G   G   :]

You can amuse yourself endlessly, by taking this progression and "plugging in" all kinds of one or two-measure licks (or *phrases* if you prefer that term), and see what combinations you come up with. It's suggested that you buy a book of 5-line banjo Tab/manuscript paper, write down some combinations of licks, and see what works. Some licks work better together than others, but you will only find out through trial and error as to what is awkward, versus what flows effortlessly.

In the pages that follow, you will find some examples of how to piece these various licks together to fit the chord changes for this progression. It's like assembling Lego Blocks!

Assembling Licks for a "G Progression"

By Jeff Belding

5 G   (G Arpeggio) pink   C   (C Arpeggio) pink

D (Lick) ring ind   D (Lick) mid ind ring   G (Lick) ring   G (Lick)

TH I M I TH   M I TH I M

6 G (Lick) ind mid   G (Lick)   C   (C)

TH I   TH I

D7   ring lift   D (Lick) mid ind   Barre * pink------------   G   (G)

(*Or ring)

Your Turn to Start Experimenting

Now you have some homework to take on. Try moving the licks around to other locations in the song; matching them to the appropriate chords. As you try out your new combinations, watch out for awkward shifts, doubling the same string on two consecutive eighth notes, or anything that "just doesn't sound quite right."

Many of the most awkward spots are the transitions between the end of one round of eight measures and the beginning of the next eight measures. Before you try a completely different lick to smooth out a rough passage, often there is a simpler fix. Sometimes, just by switching one open string with another, you can turn an awkward passage into something that works just fine, without affecting the harmony of the chord at hand.

You'll find these simple "repairs" in several places where the middle (M) finger played two eighth notes in a row. The middle finger was just switched to the index (I) finger on the second string and the problem was solved with this one-note change.

As with *all* music study, the end is merely a new beginning. Until we meet again…

GLOSSARY OF TERMS

A lot of music-oriented terminology has been thrown around in this book. This glossary should help to clear up some of the "Wait! What?" moments that may have given you pause. Some of the terms were introduced in Volume 1, and are referenced here in Volume 2.

Accompaniment—Accompaniment is the chord part for the person "backing up" a singer or soloist. Chapter 7 of Volume 1 covered basic banjo accompaniment.

Accompaniments are based on the chord structure or chord progression of a tune; these two terms being synonymous. To some extent, it is assumed that the banjoist or a guitarist can play a basic accompaniment by looking at the chords printed above the tablature staff.

Most of the tunes in this book come with enhanced or embellished banjo accompaniments. These include sparse use of banjo rolls, walk-downs, walk-ups, and other "ditties" to add interest and keep the accompanist from falling asleep!

Synonyms for accompaniment include *rhythm banjo* and *back-up banjo*. Back-up is the more commonly-used term regarding accompaniment.

One of the major challenges facing novice instrumentalists, is "switching gears" from melody into back-up (accompaniment) and back into soloing.

Accent Mark (>)—Accent marks are used in music to show the notes where a little more emphasis should be given (i.e., picked a little harder). These appear above the Tab staff in Variation 1 of "Red Wing" as a way of helping the player recognize where the melody notes are placed within the roll patterns and filler notes.

Arpeggio—An arpeggio is a "broken up" chord, played one note at a time. One of the characteristic sounds of the banjo is the use of arpeggios. Your Forward/Backward roll on open strings is a textbook case of a G major chord arpeggio. You may ask, "What is *NOT* an arpeggio?" The famous "Pinch" on your banjo is a great example, because it is two (sometimes three) notes of a chord that sound *simultaneously* rather than separately.

Back-up—Back-up is another term for *accompaniment*. The chords above all the tunes you are learning are there so a guitarist or *any* instrumentalist can back you up (it is also referred to as "playing rhythm"). No discussion of back-up is complete without mentioning play your back-ups *QUIETLY*.

BPM—BPM stands for "beats per minute." It is the standard measurement derived from the numbers on a metronome. In general, one click of the metronome represents one quarter note. If a metronome is set at 60, then it is at "60 BPM" or the same amount of time it takes the second hand to go once around your watch!

"Chops"—*Chops* is a term referring to a standard type of bluegrass back-up. The accompanist plays short, clipped chords on beats 2 and 4 of a measure (*a.k.a.* playing on the "back beat"). In a bluegrass band, the banjo or the mandolin often use this accompaniment technique.

Chord Progression—A chord progression is a series of chords that *progress* from one chord to the next. It is the foundation that gives a song or instrumental its underlying structure. For more on chord progressions, see Volume 1, pages 48–50.

A chord progression might be as simple as a four- to eight-measure series of chords that may repeat over and over for an entire song, such as "Bile Dem Cabbage Down." Many instrumentals have two distinct sections, labeled the "A Part" and "B Part." These two sections have their own unique chord progressions, but are each subsets of the structure of an entire tune.

In Chapter 5, there is a tune presented titled, "A Minor Madness." The initial material put forth in this tune (and others to follow), is learning the *chord structure*. The term *chord structure* is just a synonym for a *chord progression.* By learning the chord structure initially, you are given the building blocks for the tune's melody, variations, solos, and ideas for your own improvisations on a chord progression!

Chord Structure—See "Chord Progression."

Chord Symbols—Chord symbols are the letters that appear above the melody of the Tab staff. They serve two main purposes:

- They provide the information for an accompanist (such as guitar or mandolin) to back you up on your solos.

- In most cases, but not all, they tell the banjo player what chord to *hold in place* while playing a measure or section of a tune. In those other situations, the chord symbol implies what chord the banjoist is representing when playing a "D lick" or "G fill" or "walk-up" or other such maneuvers that function within the chord framework (i.e. the chord would not be held in place during these licks or
- fills).

Drone String—The drone string on a banjo is the fifth string. In G tuning (so far, your tuning of choice), the drone string is a high G note. It is a *constant* in that it doesn't get fretted very often, and it is used in conjunction with many chords, even if it is not an *official* part of a particular chord.

Fill—A fill is a series of notes that "fill in" the spaces between the main melody of a song. In Volume 1 page 48, Exercise 9, G fill #1 was presented for the first time and, in this Volume, G fill #2 was presented on page 52. Either of these two G fills occur most often near the end of a section of a song, and they are totally interchangeable.

Sometimes the two G fills can occur one after the other if the amount of G chord measure space permits.

What is the difference between a fill and a lick? From the author's standpoint, a fill is more of a one-measure "event" for whatever chord is at hand. A lick can be a two or more-measure occurrence, and sometimes can involve two or more chords. That's this picker's opinion anyway!

Filler Notes—Filler notes are added notes that are used when transforming a basic melody for a song into a banjo solo arrangement.

- Filler notes can be anything from an added banjo roll on the chord at hand, or an actual fill like G fill #1 or #2, as mentioned previously.

- When it comes to determining filler notes, the chord is King!

G Major Scale—The G major scale consists of the following eight notes from lowest pitch to highest: G - A - B - C - D - E - F# - G. It follows the general characteristics of *any* major scale, including the familiar sound of "Do - Re - Mi - Fa - Sol - La - Ti - Do."

Half Step—A half step is the distance between two chosen notes that are directly next to each other, and thus have no other notes in between them. When moving in half steps on your banjo, you are moving literally one fret to the next. Some examples of moving a half step on your banjo are as follows:

- Moving from first string, 4th fret F# to first string, 5th fret, high G.

- Starting at second string, open B, and moving to second string, first fret C. B and C are right next to each other fret-wise, and therefore have no sharp (or flat) note in-between them.

Harmonics (*a.k.a.* "Chimes")—Harmonics are a banjo "effect" achieved by lightly touching a string above the metal fret wire of a fret. The string is not pushed down. They are almost exclusively played at the 12th, 7th, and 5th frets. For examples of great uses of harmonics listen to any version of "Bugle Call Rag" or "Foggy Mountain Chimes."

High 2-Note C Chord—This version of a C chord found in the "banjo stratosphere," is two fingers placed on the second and first strings at the 13th and 14th frets simultaneously. It is one octave above your "regular" two-note C chord. Try doing the math from the frets of your regular C chord (the octave above any note is 12 frets higher on that string):

- First string, 2nd fret: $2 + 12 = ?$

- Second string, 1st fret: $1 + 12 = ?$

Legato—Legato means *long*—holding a note for its absolute full value, before moving on to the next note.

Lick(s)—A lick is one or more measures of notes that work well in conjunction with the chord that is called for in a particular section of music. The *same* lick can occur multiple times within a song. Sometimes a lick can come directly from another song's melody when used in an improvised solo. The use of a lick in this manner, is often referred to as a "quote."

- Some licks are notes chosen directly from the chord at hand, or a series of chord notes and scale notes that belong in the "realm" of that particular chord.

- A common synonym for lick is "phrase."

Major Chord—A major chord is a "happy-sounding" chord. An obvious example of a major chord is your G chord on all open strings. Any major chord comes from its companion major scale of the same name. It contains the first, third and fifth notes of its companion major scale. In the case of the G major scale, those three notes extracted for the G major chord are G, B, and D (note #'s 1, 3 and 5).

Major Scale—A major scale is a scale of eight notes. The first and last notes of *any* major scale are the same letter name, one octave apart in pitch from each other. The sound of a major scale is that very familiar sound of "Do - Re - Mi - Fa - Sol - La - Ti - Do." That sound is achieved by separating the consecutive notes of the scale with a specific series of whole steps and half steps (to be more fully explained in Volume 3).

Melodic Banjo—Melodic banjo is a style of playing in which each consecutive note of a phrase or lick is fretted on a different string, alternating with open strings, and also picked with a different finger than the previous note. Bill Keith was one of the early innovators of this style of playing. When executed properly, melodic style phrases have a smooth, legato flow to them, even at very fast tempos.

Melodic Run—A melodic run is a series of notes that sound more "scale-like" than typical banjo rolls or fills. These runs are played in the melodic style using carefully coordinated picking-hand and fretting-hand fingers.

Melody—The melody is the principal part of a song or instrumental with which the listener identifies or "sings along." It starts at or near the beginning of a tune, or after a short introduction (*a.k.a.* intro).

• The melodies in this book appear under several different but synonymous terms, such as, EZ Melody, Basic Melody, Basic Version (of the melody), Version 1 (of the melody), not to mention just plain-old Melody.

Minor Chord—The minor chord is a "sad-sounding" chord. It is often used in songs with a darker and more melancholy theme like "Little Sadie." An example of a widely-used minor chord is A minor (Amin). Any minor chord comes from its companion *natural minor scale* of the same name. In this case, that would be the A natural minor scale: A - B - C - D - E - F - G - A. The A minor chord consists of the first, third and fifth notes of this A natural minor scale, which are A, C and E (Note #'s 1, 3 and 5).

Movable Chord Shapes—Movable chord shapes are taking "known" chords and moving those fingerings to different parts of the neck to get a chord with a new letter name using the exact same finger combination. Examples:

• The "F chord shape" (1st, 2nd, and 3rd frets) becomes a new version of G at the 3rd, 4th, and 5th frets.

• The "D chord shape" (2nd, 3rd and 4th frets) becomes a new version of G at the 7th, 8th and 9th frets.

• The "barre shape"—2nd fret: A
                 5th fret: C
                 7th fret: D
                 12th fret: G

• The "A minor Shape" (1st and 2nd frets) becomes a new version of D minor at the 6th and 7th frets, AND a new version of E minor at the 8th and 9th frets.

• The "F minor shape" (1st and 3rd frets) becomes a new version of A minor at the 5th and 7th frets.

• The full explanation of where these various chord names come from will be forthcoming in Volume 3.

Music Theory—Music Theory is the subject that embodies *all* explanations as to the why behind any aspect of music. It is the set of many rules for music regarding various subsets of subjects such as scales, chords, chord progressions, tuning, and harmony, just to name a few. It is the "science" behind what makes music "tick." So, you might say it's not really just Music Theory, it's Music *FACT!*

Octave—An octave describes a pitch that bears the same letter name as the note higher or lower in pitch than your starting point note. If you were to start at third string, open G, your next higher octave G note (the note that bears the same letter name) is fifth string, open *or* first string, 5th fret.

• The lowest pitch on your banjo (at least in your current G tuning) is fourth string, open D. The next higher octave D note is *first* string, open D.

We have also become aware of a fretted note on the first string, 4th fret, an F#. The octave *lower* F# is located at the *fourth* string, 4th fret.

"The next octave higher" of a G major scale, *starts* on the high G or fifth string open, and continues up from there, incorporating the higher A and B notes from your "9/10 position" (Volume 1, Pages 36 and 37). A *full* octave higher G scale is possible, but was not used in this book because of the "higher" (pun intended) difficulty of playing that complete octave-higher G scale.

Open String—An open string is any string that is picked with your picking hand, but is not pressed down or fretted with your fretting hand. The names of the open strings of the banjo when in G tuning are (5th to 1st):

High G (5th), Low D (4th), G (3rd), B (2nd), and High D (1st)

It is highly recommended that you take the time to memorize them!

"Perceived" chords—Perceived chords occur when the banjo is capoed. They are chords seen by the capoed banjoist as *one* name, but in actuality have a *different* name based on the position where the capo is placed on the banjo neck. Chord names are perceived by fretted instrument players by their finger shapes. It takes a lot of know-how and brain twisting to call a perceived chord by its "real" name. That's why many folks at jams call chords by their numbers instead of names. Next question: "How do chords get these numbers?" Another weighty subject for another book, but here's a table to give you an idea:

Table of primary chords in your working keys, based on what is known as the "Nashville Number System":

Key of:	1 chord	4 chord	5 chord
G	G	C	D (or D7)
A	A	D	E (or E7)
C	C	F	G (or G7)
D	D	G	A (or A7)

Pick-ups—The term pick-ups is short for *pick-up notes*. Pick-ups refer to one to several introductory notes that start off a tune in an "incomplete measure." That is a *short* measure which leads the player into the first complete measure of a tune. For "Turkey in the Straw" the basic version shows a two-note pick-up measure. Pick-up notes are also in the last measure of each accompaniment section of that tune. Notice you are instructed to play those pick-ups *only* on the *second* time through the back-up for the B part.

Primary Chords of a Key—The primary chords of a key are the three *main* chords found in a particular piece of music, at least 90% of the time. Each different key has its own set of primary chords. The primary chords for the key of G are G, C, and D (interchangeable with D7), for the key of A they are A, D, and E (interchangeable with E7), for the key of C they are C, F, and G and for the key of D they are D, G, A. Why these chords? It would take scores *of pages* rather than a paragraph to explain it fully. For now, I highly recommend you memorize these four sets of chords. This knowledge will come in handy at bluegrass jams.

Keep in mind that *minor* keys (as opposed to m*aj*or keys like G, A, and C) have their *own* sets of primary chords - another theoretical can of worms to "open" someday. Also keep in mind that music composers don't *have to* use these primary chords in their compositions under penalty of law! That's why I mentioned 90%. In the other 10% of musical composing *ANYTHING GOES!*

Repeat Previous Measure Symbol (%)—The repeat previous measure symbol means exactly what it says. Whatever you played in the previous measure must be played over *again.* If a *second* symbol appears in the next measure, then all of that information must be repeated yet *again.* Granted, the percent symbol is not *exactly* what it looks like, but it's the closest you can get to it in a word processing program.

Root of a scale or chord—The root note of a scale or chord refers to the first ("1") note of *any* scale (major, minor, or otherwise). The term root also refers to the note within any *chord* which gives the chord its name. Therefore, the root is the namesake of a scale or chord.

Scale fragment—A scale fragment is three to five notes of a scale (major or minor), and is played to create a lick that goes with the chord at hand.

Solo—The term solo can have several usages. A solo can be the main part in an ensemble of players. In bluegrass, each player gets the opportunity to be a soloist. In a typical song, a solo is usually taken after a verse and chorus are sung.

- A banjo solo is taking the basic melody of a tune and adding licks, fills, and filler notes to give that melody a "banjoistic" treatment. One example of this is in Chapter 8 using the basic version of the melody of "Red Wing" to flesh out a banjo solo.

- This term also refers to the *improvised* solo. This kind of solo, be it banjo or any other instrument, does not have to have *anything* to do with a song's melody. It is a matter of using the song's chord structure or chord progression to create an off-the-cuff solo that (hopefully) "flows like a stream" through the chord progression.

- Can a solo be the same as an EZ or Basic Melody? Absolutely! When the leader of a bluegrass jam looks at *you* and says, "Take it!", use whatever knowledge you have from the most basic melody to the craziest variation that you can conjure up. It's *your* moment. *You* are in charge, so by all means, "Take it!"

Stratosphere—The Stratosphere refers to any place on the neck from the 12th to the 22nd fret.

Syncopated (or noun, Syncopation)—Syncopation is the musical term for a change in the timing of a melody. A melody becomes syncopated when it "breaks away" with a different accent from the normal rhythm it is played. An eighth note immediately followed by a quarter note is one example of syncopation. It fools the listener into thinking that the timing of a melody is off, but before long it brings the listener back to reality by eventually getting the timing on track. Banjoist Roger Sprung is a master of syncopation. If you want a good example of this technique, listen to his version of "Dill Pickle Rag" or even his own version of "Red Wing."

Tacet—Tacet means silent. In other words, don't play. It may show up at the ending of a tune when the accompaniment is supposed to stop for the banjo to play an ending lick.

Tag *a.k.a.* Ending—This is a series of two to four measures that punctuate a song or instrumental. In the case of a vocal song, it involves repeating the last line of a chorus to bring the song home to its conclusion. For an instrumental, it is anything from a simple "Shave and a Haircut" ending, to an elaborate set of chosen notes to put the final touch on the tune. In a jam, the leader of a song will often "put their foot up" to let everyone else know that the Tag is on the way in very short order.

"Taters"—"Taters" are a series of repetitive rhythmic licks that are used to set the tempo of a song or tune in order to give it a smooth start-up. At first used by fiddle players, they were soon adapted to the banjo in their own unique way. In this book they are presented to start off a song in the key of G (*or* key of A with a capo).

Transpose—The act of transposing means to take a particular melody and its chords and play the same melody and its chords in a different key. Your first example of transposing a tune was to take the tune "Cripple Creek" originally played in G and *transpose* the tune to the key of A, using the capo as a tool for *easy* transposition.

It is also possible to transpose a melody *directly* without the use of a capo, but it requires a detailed knowledge of *every* note's position on the banjo neck—a lifetime's worth of study, but well worth it if you wish to take the time to do so.

"Up the Neck"—"Up the Neck" refers to any lick (phrase) or chord that is played from basically the 5th fret through the 12th fret and even beyond. There is a common erroneous discrepancy of going up to the higher numbered frets and referring to such a maneuver as "going down the neck." From a visual stand-point, that may be true, but we are not concerned with what it *looks* like. We are going up the neck to get to the *higher pitched* notes. If this is hard to grasp when looking at your banjo neck, then just consider the fact that you are moving to higher *numbered* frets. It's all about *pitch*.

Variation(s)—A variation is any solo that is an embellishment of the basic melody to a tune. The idea of variations comes from a classical music form known as, "Theme and Variations." Most of the tunes in this book are presented in this musical form. They start with a basic melody (*a.k.a.* EZ Melody, Basic Version or Version 1), and then are followed up with one to four variations, each one being progressively more challenging than the previous.

Walk-up—The walk-up is a brief scale of notes used in place of a chord that provide a musical bridge between sections of a tune. You will find walk-ups in both 4/4 time *and* waltzes. They add interest to back-up playing and often serve as a place-keeper as to where you are in a song.

Waltz—A waltz is a specific type of dance rhythm that is *always* in 3/4 (three-quarter) time. Some well-known examples of waltz-rhythm songs are "All the Good Times," "Dark as a Dungeon," "Ashokan Farewell" and "The Beautiful Blue Danube."

Whole Step—A whole step in general, refers to the space between two particular notes. This space between these two notes *always* has one note (or one *fret*) in-between that is skipped over or "left out" to get from the first note to the next one—a whole step away. For comparison's sake, see "Half Step." Some examples of moving a whole step on your banjo are as follows:

- Moving from first string, open D, to first string, 2nd fret, E. The first fret is that "left-out note" in-between those *two notes* you want in your whole step move from D to E (for your information, that first fret note is D#).

- Moving from fourth string, 2nd fret E to fourth string, 4th fret F#. This maneuver often occurs as part of a walk-up. You need E and F#, and you *skip* the fourth string, 3rd fret (regular or natural F) to make that move.

- Also, keep in mind that the movement of a whole step (going *up* in pitch) is from one alphabetical letter to the very *next* letter (not to mention that sometimes you land on a sharp). A whole step going *down* in pitch is going backwards to the previous alphabetical letter. This kind of movement works for chords as well.

About the Author

Jeff Belding studied at The New England Conservatory and The College of Saint Rose, where he received a Bachelor's Degree in Studio Music. He studied banjo extensively with Roger Sprung, who mentored and inspired him to become a music instructor himself, teaching banjo, guitar and other stringed instruments in Upstate New York.

Continuing studies on banjo with Bill Keith, lead Jeff to further his knowledge of Music Theory and its application to the instrument. It is in the spirit of passing on some of this knowledge of the late, great Bill Keith to other banjo pickers, that Jeff continues to teach and write about music.

Jeff's lifelong career in music has given him a diverse background in bluegrass, country, rock, jazz and classical music styles. He has performed on the banjo for a multitude of studio projects including: Frank Gadler's (of NRBQ) most recent solo record *Cause of You,* The Willie Amrod Band CD *Everywhere Is Outta Town*, Vito Petroccitto Jr's *The Yankee Song* (25th Anniversary Edition), Lise Winne's *Winged with Hopes* CD and many others.

Since the age of nine in 1965, Jeff knew that music was his calling. Five decades later, Jeff continues to spread his knowledge of music and bluegrass banjo in the form of this book (Volume Two) and two prior books, *New Techniques For 5 String Banjo, Volume 1* and *12 Songs Of Christmas, Duets for 5 String Banjo and Guitar* (all available for purchase from amazon.com).

He currently lives in Mesa, Arizona where he can be found playing at local jams, blogging and pursuing a career as an author and composer.

One of Jeff's fondest memories was winning first place in the "New Twists For Banjo" original tune contest in the 1980's, judged by Tony Trischka. You can read all about it at www.jeffbelding.com.

www.ingramcontent.com/pod-product-compliance
Lightning Source LLC
Chambersburg PA
CBHW062051090426

42740CB00016B/3098